BAIT

By
Donald E. Stephen

Tales Press
Urbana, Illinois

Second Edition, 2001 by Tales Press, Urbana, Illinois
First Edition, 1986
© Copyright 2001 by Donald E. Stephen
Cover sketch by Linda Miller
Cover design by Carlton Bruett

Library of Congress Cataloging-in-Publication Data

Stephen, Donald E.
  Bait / by Donald E. Stephen.-- 2nd ed.
     p. cm.
  ISBN 0-9641423-5-X
  1. Vietnamese Conflict, 1961-1975--Personal narratives, American. 2.
Stephen, Donald E. I. Title.
  DS559.6 .S74 2001
  959.704'3'092--dc21

                          2001004600

Acknowledgments

A very special thanks to my brother, Paul, without whose encouragement and help, this book would never have been published.

I thank also my wife, Barbara, artist Linda Miller of Martinsville, Illinois, for the design and artwork of the cover, and editors Ray Elliott and Vanessa Faurie for their efforts in getting the revised edition published.

In Memory of
Michael M. Dalton
August 15, 1946 — June 9, 1971

I have dedicated this book to Mike. He was the epitome of devotion to the basic principles that have made this country what it is today. Mike was not only a friend in Vietnam, but also a young man whom I admired and respected. The purpose of writing this book is to keep our experience before the public; perhaps people will better understand that the thousands killed and wounded in Vietnam did not die in vain or lose a limb for nothing.

Whether a person considers Vietnam a victory or a loss is irrelevant. Young men and women gave everything for a principle that I hope all Americans would be proud to support. Freedom is not something one can give or take on a whim. It has been fought for and bought with the blood of our youth.

There are many thoughts that Mike and I exchanged over many hours of conversation. The one expression that meant very much to us was: "Freedom, for those who have fought for it, has a meaning the protected will never know."

So to Mike Dalton, and also to Floyd Kotewa, Wheeler, Jackson, Colonel Sutton, and those of the Third, 187th, who gave their lives for the principle of freedom, I dedicate these pages.

Prologue

The information in this book is true; each incident I experienced in Vietnam happened as described. Although I may have the wrong names involved at times, the incidents did occur and are told from my perspective as a lieutenant. Each individual I served with could add his own view. It was not my intention to place any person in a false time or place. For this I ask the people with whom I served to bear with me. I praise the men in Second Platoon, for I owe my life to them. We were a team with common goals, and I'm proud to have served with every man.

This book started as a sort of journal which helped me take a lot of problems out of my mind and put them on paper. After much encouragement from friends, I decided to finish the manuscript so that the public could share in a private time of my life.

It is imperative to realize that a platoon was not put together with men who came in-country on the same day. From the day I took over as platoon leader, men began going home, and there were very few replacements. Most of them were eighteen years old or just turning nineteen. I was the oldest in Second Platoon, and I turned twenty-five in September 1971. As I recall, other than Sergeant Cuevas, almost all of the men were under twenty. Since that time I've had two sons turn eighteen, and it's been very difficult for me to imagine them in the same situation. I'm sure they would have done our country proud, but I now understand how parents feel about sending their children off to war.

I have read many books on Vietnam, and I'm not saying that they are wrong or misquoted, but I do feel the need to point out that many veterans have come home and adjusted to society. There are many problems connected to the Vietnam era. Each individual must face those problems in his own way. We cannot change society by a simple monument or legislation. Those of us who survived this era of history must, at all cost, fight for our rights so that our comrades did not die in vain.

One other point needs to be stressed regarding the infantry "grunt" who survived the jungle. If the enemy and the booby traps were taken away, mere survival in the jungle would have been traumatic enough for most young men. The average ruck-sack weighed between eighty and one hundred pounds. The temperature ranged from ninety to one hundred degrees, day and night. Insects were always present; horseflies and greenheads bit men unrelentingly.

There were poisonous snakes. Bee stings were frequent. Some of the men were bitten by rodents. Leeches were a night-mare in most of the areas.

A rain could last for days with no let up. Immersion foot was a constant problem; cellulitis from the least scratch caused pain to nerve endings. In most cases, the jungle rotted off our clothes in three weeks from constant sweat and wear. Venereal disease from R-and-R personnel was another problem.

Contact with the outside world was made through a door gunner on a resupply helicopter. Sometimes weeks would go by with no word from home, and then suddenly, the backlog of mail would be there. Tim "Tex" Lissenbee's father died. I can only imagine the thoughts Tex had; leaving the jungle for the funeral, then returning to the jungle and the war.

"Dear John" letters, homesickness, and fear were daily problems I had to handle as a lieutenant. Military protocol made things extremely difficult when surviving the jungle was the only thing that mattered.

I cannot easily forgive those who refused to serve our country. We have had deserters in every war, and all were given amnesty. But I cannot forgive those who consider they did nothing wrong. I am an American citizen, proud of my heritage, and proud to have served as a soldier. The right or wrong of the Vietnam War is not my burden. I was called and I served.

To my lifelong friends of the Third, 187th: I salute you and look forward to hearing from anyone who was there.

—Donald E. Stephen
3733 E. Snake Trail Rd.
Martinsville, IL 62442

1

I was commissioned a second lieutenant in February 1970. Afterwards, I immediately enrolled in jump school where I parachuted out of five airplanes. I made seven more jumps in Special Forces training.

At the time of my departure for Vietnam I was twenty-four years old. I had jumped out of more planes than I had landed in, so it may seem silly to say that I didn't like flying and wasn't looking forward to an eighteen-hour flight. I'd never been airsick to the extent of vomiting, but I was uncomfortable all the time.

I arrived in New Jersey at McGuire Air Force Base at about one in the afternoon after spending a thirty-day leave at home in eastern Illinois. It took thirty minutes to process our orders. The plane was ready. There were approximately two hundred of us who boarded.

I sat down with two captains. One was an old enlisted veteran who had become a chaplain, and the other was a young career captain going to Vietnam for his third tour of duty. Luckily, I got the aisle seat, which made my discomfort a little more bearable, knowing I could run to the john if I needed to.

When I heard the big door close and saw the seat belt light flash, I knew I was headed into a world which I wasn't sure I could handle.

Our plane was in the air one hour when the pilot outlined our flight plan. Our first stop was to be Anchorage,
Alaska, for refueling, but after our supper of roast beef and
a few drinks, the pilot came back and said that Anchorage
was fogged in and we would be staying in Seattle for the
night. A large cheer went up from everyone.

In Seattle, there were military police who escorted us to
rooms and stayed with us all night. They even stayed outside
the latrine. They were armed with pistols, handcuffs, and night
sticks. I couldn't believe that we had to be guarded so closely,
but apparently several men had let the fear of war get to them
and they had tried to run even after the trip had started.

I only saw a few square feet of Seattle under the circumstances, but maybe someday I'll be able to see it during the
day. It sure looked pretty at night.

The next day, after a breakfast of roast beef (because of
the weather which fouled up military supply) we landed in
Anchorage at about 10:30. Again, the military police were there,
and heavily armed. They had even painted lines for us to walk
between.

We had approximately one hour to buy gifts or souvenirs.
I thought it was kind of ridiculous because I didn't know what
I was going to do with a lot of souvenirs to pack around for a
year.

We changed pilots and stewardesses in Anchorage. On the
way to Japan, they served dinner. Roast beef again. In Japan,
we had about an hour in the terminal, and again, we were
watched very closely. Even in the latrine, there were bars on
the windows.

We had one more stop before reaching Vietnam. I'm not
sure what island we landed on, but it was a small one, and the
military police weren't nearly as strict because there was no
place to go. I'm pretty sure we changed pilots there and flew to
Long Binh, which is a suburb of Saigon. While in flight, we
received one more meal of airplane roast beef, and there were a

few heated words about that meal. I wasn't complaining because I'd only eaten about a tenth of the food, so I really didn't care what was served.

The pilot explained that we would be landing just before dark. We learned that no planes had been bombed or sabotaged for two weeks, but that was no consolation. I was concerned about one flight only—ours.

It was cold in Illinois when I left home. It was cold in New Jersey, Washington, and Alaska, mild in Japan, and warm on the island. I was wearing full-dress Army green. When I stepped off the plane in Long Binh, the heat and humidity almost caused me to pass out. I could hardly breathe.

They loaded us onto buses, which had bars on the windows, as well as screen wire. This time it was to protect us from the enemy, instead of to prevent escape. By then it was dark and we drove for about thirty minutes through the worst slums imaginable. They would have made Chicago look good. It was really spooky driving through this area.

I was sweating to the point that my underwear was wet. I loosened my tie and tried to keep from looking outside the windows, but I couldn't, and I remember thinking that old Don was really somewhere he hadn't planned on being.

After the bus ride, we checked into a bunking area for the night, and it was about midnight when we got settled. The barracks had plywood floors, plywood walls about four feet high, and then screen the rest of the way up, with one-by-four-inch louvers for air passage.

At 3 A.M., the Dallas Cowboys, my football team, were in the Super Bowl, and we all sat around and listened. I'm not a real football nut, but I think Dallas lost in the last seconds of the game. If I'm wrong, I apologize to Dallas. It just shows how a person's memory fails over the years.

The next morning we shipped our clothes home and were issued jungle fatigues, which helped me a great deal. Several classes were presented to us concerning our attitudes as officers, and we were given a breakdown of the country. Vietnam was broken down into four corps areas. The I Corps Area was north and the IV Corps Area was south. We were presented with dream sheets and were told to circle five units to which we would like to be assigned.

It was 1971. A captain gave me a word of advice. He told me not to ask for anything in the I Corps Area, so I circled five choices as close to Saigon as possible. I got the I Corps Area anyway. That's why it was called a dream sheet.

It was during this three-day period that I realized I had been the only second lieutenant on the airplane. Everyone else was either a captain, major, or warrant officer. I didn't know how many people came in-country on a given day or where they were all processed, but I had a feeling that there ought to have been more than one green second lieutenant.

On the second day, a special class was held on drug abuse in Vietnam. At the end of the class, a mild form of marijuana was passed out to every one of us. We were told to light the joint and smoke it if we wanted. The purpose was to let us know what it smelled like.

For three months prior to OCS (Officer Candidate School), I'd been assigned to a holdover platoon in Fort Gordon, Georgia. While I was there, I saw many types of drug use, from sucking shoe dye poured over a sock, to every pill imaginable, so I knew what grass smelled like.

I'd never smoked before, nor taken any other kind of drug, so I didn't try my cigarette that day. I sat and watched captains and majors light up. They enjoyed every bit of the grass.

Not all of the officers partook, and several did as I, and refused even to light up. Still, I thought, these are the people who are going to lead men into combat.

My mind clicked and stored the incident. I'd have to check out my superior officers closely. It was going to be a long year for this country boy.

On the third day, I crawled on a C-130 for Da Nang. There

were privates through sergeants on this plane. I was the only butter-bar (nickname for second lieutenants because the gold bar looked like the color of butter) aboard. I Corps is in the northern part of South Vietnam, so I had to go from Saigon in the south to Da Nang. There, we transferred to a shit-hook (Chinook) and flew to a place in the north called Phu Bai, the finance center for the 101st Air Mobile.

We spent two days there, and the rumors were flying hot and heavy. The biggest one was that the war was almost over. It was only off by about four years. One saying which we heeded was, "Enjoy your hot shower because it might be your last."

Up to this point, no one had issued me a weapon of any kind or even talked about weapons. We boarded deuce-and-a-half trucks and headed north toward a place called Camp Evans. When we drove through the town of Phu Bai, we had to go slowly at times, and the little kids would run up to the truck and ask for money, candy, or anything we wanted to give. If they could grab a man's wrist, his watch was gone in a flash.

It took about forty-five minutes to reach Camp Evans. During that time, I began to realize that, with each passing mile, I was getting farther and farther away from civilization, and closer and closer to the war.

Upon arriving at Evans, the convoy wound around through two or three company areas to a place on the southeast perimeter. We were greeted by a large sign that read SERTS, and I knew it couldn't have been a candy mint.

After billeting in, I met several officers. All were either captains or warrant officers, and, sure enough, I was the only second lieutenant there. I remember it being very troublesome being the junior officer because of all the stories I'd heard about Army discipline in a combat zone.

I had problems the first day because I didn't know who to salute and who not to salute. Some got mad if I saluted them and some got mad if I didn't, so I quickly remembered to differentiate between the two groups. It worked the same for me, except I didn't get mad either way, and I hoped the enlisted men didn't hold any grudges against me. I sure knew how they felt because I had been a draftee before going to officers' school.

I'm not really sure what SERTS stood for, but I think it meant Screaming Eagle Replacement Training School; however, its true meaning was expressed in one sentence: "Wake up boy, you are now in a war zone and this is your last chance to learn before the checker game starts." I won't easily forget that week of training. We pulled bunker guard the first night, and I, being the only lieutenant, got the sublime honor of officer of the day and night for six whole days.

I found it hard to believe that everyone but myself had a weapon on guard duty. SERTS commanded seventeen bunkers on the perimeter, and each was filled with a "newby," or "cherry," or "new-man-in-the-country." Every one of us was scared to death because the inner feeling of security just wasn't there. If there had been a few veterans among us, it would have been a lot easier.

In front of each bunker there were Claymore mines, fougasse (a mixture of diesel fuel and gas), and plenty of wire. It was not uncommon for the enemy to penetrate the wire. If we saw or heard anything, we had permission to fire immediately; however, the proper procedure was to notify the officer of the day to get a second opinion. But the area was filled with cherries who were either too cautious or too scared, so anything was liable to happen.

Stateside (in the U.S.A.), the officer of the day got a jeep which he drove to make his rounds while posting the guard and checking on all the positions. In SERTS, however, they issued me a mule. Actually, it was a flat-bed trailer approximately four by six feet with rubber tires and a steering wheel. They were called mules, and they were pretty handy, except they had no lights. When a man drove around the bunker system after dark to talk to some new-men-in-country, it was quite an experience. But it was a lot better to drive at night in a noisy mule than to walk quietly and have some scared individual shoot if he heard a twig snap.

There was a hootch set up in the middle of the compound where movies were shown each night, so, in between bunker rounds, we would drive up to the movie shack and watch for a little while. On the third night, as I approached the movie hootch, I saw someone peeking through the louvers. As I got closer, he turned and said "*Chou hoi*," and I nearly shit my pants because he was Vietnamese.

"What in the Sam Hill are you doing here?" I yelled in surprise.

Now remember, I didn't have a weapon, and I didn't speak Vietnamese. He did have his arms in the air, but it was dark and I didn't understand the language, so I jumped on him and wrestled him to the ground, and all he could do was repeat "*Chou hoi, chou hoi!*" I was only five-feet-eight and one hundred pounds, but he was five feet and one hundred pounds, so I won the struggle because he didn't fight back. I pinned his hands behind his back and frisked him from top to bottom, and then we headed for the command post. When I shoved the little man through the door, the sergeant nearly had a heart attack. He held a .45 pistol to the dink's head while I called the captain.

During the five minutes that followed, we searched him again and found nothing but a pocket full of tissue paper and little pieces of wire similar to paper slips. The colonel arrived with an interpreter and someone from the intelligence division. They questioned the dink and found he was from a sapper unit in North Vietnam. (Specially trained soldiers who carried out specific missions like blowing up an ammunition dump and causing other problems behind enemy lines.) He was on a mission to destroy the fuel depot at Camp Evans, but instead he'd decided to surrender. He claimed he crawled through the wire about dark, and this was about 2 A.M. He had been walking around trying to find someone to surrender to, but couldn't quite figure out how to go about it.

When he saw the movie going on, he was fascinated because he had never seen one before, and that was when I caught him. He said I was a very strong, mean soldier.

Finally, someone realized I was present and asked me what happened, so I explained everything, and, of course, in the light of the room and the presence of fellow soldiers, I was a lot braver. I got several handshakes and pats on the back.

The next morning we had a special class. It was a demonstration given by a real enemy soldier (the same guy) on how to sneak through heavy concertina wire and past alert American soldiers. He explained that he had trained for two years as a sapper to accomplish one mission. He had walked all the way from Laos carrying nothing but a few satchel charges, some rice, and dried fish. Then he told us he had lain outside the wire for three days covered with dried mud, crawling closer and closer each day and night until he reached our perimeter. He said it only took five minutes to get through the wire and slip past our guards. Not too many believed this, so he proved it.

Remember those pieces of paper and wire clips? Well, that little dink stripped down to his underwear and started going through that wire. He grabbed hold of two pieces of wire and clipped them together along with a piece of paper, and within minutes he was through the concertina wire, grinning at us like a possum eating shit. The small pieces of paper were to mark his escape route.

After the completion of a mission, a sapper would *di di moi*, or run like hell, back to Laos to train for another mission. He avoided all contact with people, friend or enemy, until the completion of his mission. We found out later that day, in another class, that *"Chou hoi"* means "I surrender," or words to that effect.

On the day before graduation, I was getting tired of being the only lieutenant. It was rainy, overcast, and just plain old dreary. A jeep pulled up out of the mist, and a sergeant asked for Lieutenant Stephen.

"Take me to your leader," I said, after getting up slowly. And that's just what he did. I don't remember the name of the outfit or the colonel, but I was interviewed and told they would like to have me in their outfit. I didn't know what to say, so the colonel told me to go back to SERTS and think on it.

About forty-five minutes after returning, another jeep pulled up asking for Lieutenant Stephen. I crawled in, and away we went to another battalion, and another colonel I didn't know.

I returned to SERTS, and some of the captains and warrant officers razzed me about being the most wanted lieutenant in Vietnam. I told them I didn't know about being wanted, but I sure felt used and that I'd be glad when I did get to my unit.

The next morning, after guard duty was over, I got into bed, and about thirty minutes into my first good sleep, somebody shook me awake and said there was a jeep outside waiting for me. This time it was only minutes to the battalion area. I met Colonel Sutton and was immediately impressed with the man. We talked for quite a while, and he told me he had priority over me, but he would prefer it if I volunteered to join his unit.

I should have known right then that something big was up, but being green, it didn't soak in. However, of the three colonels, I felt most comfortable with Colonel Sutton, so I said as much, and told him I would be glad to become a member of the Rakkasans.

That was January 18, 1971, I think, but I could be off a day or two. I retired to SERTS and packed my belongings. At 4:30 P.M., I left for the Third Battalion, 187th Infantry, 101st Airborne—a pacification unit.

2

A jeep pulled into the SERTS compound and picked me up, along with three privates. The Third Battalion, 187th, was almost within a stone's throw, but we drove the distance anyway. We all signed into battalion headquarters where we were assigned a company.

I walked down to Delta Company, which was at the end of the compound, and signed in there also. There I met Captain Edwards, my new company commander, and said goodbye to Lieutenant Baniseck, whom I was replacing. He acted as if he was in a hurry to leave, so I didn't get a chance to talk to him about the men in the platoon.

By then it was about five in the evening. The captain told me to go down to S-4 (supply) and get all my supplies because there would be a briefing at six o'clock. Sergeant Cuevas came in at about that time and announced he was Second Platoon sergeant, and said that I'd been assigned to his platoon.

He told me he had signed in only a week ago and that this was his third tour of duty. It made me feel good to know that I had an experienced platoon sergeant.

He then told me he was supposed to have a desk job in Saigon and that he wasn't very happy about being in the I Corps Area. He said something big was coming and he didn't know what, but he would have no part of it. He had been wounded twice and wasn't taking any chances for anyone. He informed me that he would not take men on patrol under any circumstances, nor would he do anything that he thought dangerous. He would order supplies and help with the platoon, but that was it.

My heart fell down to my socks, and I was glad when we reached S-4. There I met Chief Warrant Officer Hall, who issued me more stuff than I ever imagined. In all my training, I had never seen the true rucksack, or the supplies the soldier put in it.

The sergeant and I laid out all the equipment on the bed, and I told him there was no way it was going to go in that little rucksack. But Sergeant Cuevas just popped the top of his beer and said that it would. There were three days worth of C-rations (nine meals), ten quarts of water, a poncho and liner, an air mattress, ten hand grenades, 150 feet of rope, a personal can, and lots of small items. I crammed them into the ruck and tried to pick it up. It weighed between eighty and one hundred pounds. I told him that I couldn't carry it all day in addition to my weapon and ammunition. He popped a top on another beer and told me I would.

"Yours is the lightest in the platoon," he added.

I thought I was surely amidst a bunch of football linemen if they could carry all that and more.

By then it was 5:50, so I headed for the briefing room. I finally got to see several lieutenants, as well as captains and majors. A map board covered almost one whole wall. Colonel Sutton addressed our group.

"Gentlemen, at 0600 we start operation Lam Son 719. The Third, 187th, has been chosen as the spearhead battalion. The ARVNs (Army of the Republic of Vietnam) will be going into Laos. We have only three days to get the American troops in position. The main road into Laos is going to be called Red Devil Drive. Our job is to protect both sides of that road so the ARVNs have safety up to the Laotian border. Under no circumstances are we going into Laos."

We would be working areas that had been in enemy hands since 1968. Khe Sanh would be the focal point of our operation. The Marines had dug it in 1968, and it would serve as our new home during the mission. Our battalion would be the first one airlifted into the area, but many battalions would follow. We would be alone for just a short time, then the area would be saturated with American troops.

The maps were handed out, and the whole plan was developed. Several bridges had to be built in three days. They had to be protected as well. I thought it was impossible that all this was going to happen in a three-day period, but since I was only going to handle a platoon in the grand plan, I was only concerned about my position during the offensive.

We all left the briefing room and headed back for D Company. Captain Edwards told me to come by in one hour and he would explain a little more about my job, I walked back to the hootch and found it deserted, except for an enormous amount of gear and personal belongings. I didn't have any idea where everyone was, or what to do next, so I sat down on my army cot and thought about the world situation.

My first thought was that at 0600 the next day I might die, and I didn't know where I was or who I was with. Everyone was in such a hurry, at least seemed to know where they were going, and I felt like Jonah in the whale's belly. I prayed for a while; then I got my maps and compass, and I studied for about an hour until Sergeant Cuevas came in. I told him what I knew about the next day.

"Holy Mother of God!" he exclaimed and popped the top on another beer.

"I have to see the captain for more details," I said. "When I'm through there, I want to meet some or all of the platoon."

When I reported to Captain Edwards, he told me to have my platoon rucked up and on the helipad at 0500. Since there were three rifle platoons and one mortar platoon, there was always one platoon that stayed with the command post, and, since I was new, I would be the one guarding the CP until I learned the procedures. I left the captain feeling a little better. At least I wasn't going to be dropped in the middle of nowhere to fend for myself.

By then, it was 2300 hours, so Cuevas and I walked over to Second Platoon barracks. On the way, my stomach felt like it did the first time I ever stood up to speak in front of a group.

I knew that I was responsible for the men I was about to meet. One mistake could cost the lives of several men. I would have loved to have had someone close to talk to, someone to ask advice from.

God, why couldn't I have had a few days to get to know people ... at least their names, I thought.

I didn't get an answer.

The music was so loud I couldn't hear myself think. I braced myself and walked inside.

Now, if you have ever wondered what you would say to a group of men you have never seen before and you are about to become their boss, just magnify that one hundred times because of the combat situation we were in, and you might begin to see how I felt. I had heard so many stories stateside. If you were a poor leader, you could get shot in the back or "fragged" in your sleep. These were the same thoughts I would later have myself about a few officers.

What I said to them may not have been too original or too "army" but it came out nonetheless.

"I'm Don Stephen. I'm twenty-four years old. I'm a farm boy from Illinois, and I love country music. Tomorrow at 0400 we will wake up, and at 0500 be on the helipad ready to leave. I'm brand new and I have a lot to learn. I expect you to teach me, and in turn, I will teach you what I know."

I looked around and realized they were not big football players. In fact, most of them were no bigger than me. There wasn't a Dick Butkus among them, and they looked so young in their features. But their eyes were much older. I'm not sure what their eyes told that night, but I was really uncomfortable looking into them.

Some of them were playing cards, some were drinking in groups of four. I noticed that there were no sheets or pillows on any of the beds. It may seem silly to notice something like that, but so far I had associated any kind of bed with a blanket, or if nothing else, a pillow. The other thing I noticed was that several of the men had small bandages all over their arms. I would learn the reason for this later.

"Who is the RTO here?" I asked.

A young SP-4 (specialist four) by the name of Mike Daugherty stood up and said he was Lieutenant Baniseck's radio telephone operator.

"Give me your extra radio batteries, and I'll carry them in my rucksack."

He passed them to me.

"I'll work with you for a few days," he told me, "but I'm going to Captain Edwards' command post as soon as possible."

At 0130, I returned to the officers' barracks, and a few of the lieutenants were getting ready for bed. The only one I wouldn't see again was Lieutenant Cross, who was the senior lieutenant in the field. They were all about half-looped on beer and whiskey, and ready for a few short hours of sleep.

I was ready for some indoctrination from people who had been around for a while, so I asked for some advice, and one lieutenant told me to get some sleep because there were only two types of lieutenants: the quick to learn and the dead. And time would tell which I was.

Real comforting, I thought. Then Lieutenant Cross spoke:

"The only advice I can give you is to read your map carefully and be sure to know where you say you are, or not only will the enemy blow you away but so will the Americans. You can be off a few meters, but if you are a few too many, our artillery will blow you to pieces. ... Other than that, look, listen, and learn."

I found out later that Lieutenant Cross was the only one to have been under enemy fire, and then only briefly, so the rest were just as scared about the next day as I was. I lay down with my ruck for a pillow and tried to sleep.

At 0400, the light bulb in the hootch came on. I didn't know when I fell asleep, but apparently I had, and I'd slept sounder than I would for several nights to come. Everybody grabbed his toothbrush and headed for the shower area, so I followed since I didn't know where it was. Then it was off to the mess hall where someone had stayed up to fix hot chow.

I sat down across from Captain Edwards, who was a big man in comparison to the rest of us. I thought he looked awfully old for a captain. He asked me several questions about my training. I told him I'd been drafted after a divorce.

"I put in my basic at Fort Campbell, Kentucky," I said, rattling my duty stations off, "my advanced training at Fort Gordon, Georgia, my Officer Candidate School at Benning, jump school at Benning, training officer at Fort Puke, Diseaseville, Louseianna (Fort Polk, Leesville, Louisiana), and Green Beret School at Fort Bragg, North Carolina."

When I mentioned the latter, you could have heard a pin drop.

"You're a Green Beret in an infantry company?" the captain asked in disbelief.

"Well, it's a long story. When I get time, I'll tell you about it. For now, I'm in this unit, and it's hard telling where I'll end up."

"You've got a good platoon," he said, laughing, "but the Third, 187th, has been a pacification unit. They've seen very little action. I'm hoping to see plenty before this mission is over."

I thought I could do without any action for twelve months.

He told me to enjoy the food because it might be the last good chow I'd eat for a while. After tasting it, I wasn't sure there would be all that much to miss.

"Are you going to make a career out of the service?" Edwards asked.

"I don't think so," I replied. "I was a farmer before I was drafted. I still want to farm when I go home."

"Do exactly as you're told, when you're told, and we'll get along fine," he told me.

I assured him those were my intentions. I didn't know that a short time later I would not be listening to anyone but myself and a few close friends.

We all left the mess hall and headed back to the hootches. I gathered my gear and noticed that everybody had loaded their ammunition in their M-16s. A little reality set in about then, when I realized that our entire battalion was locked and loaded, and ready to kill or be killed. I put my rucksack on and could barely walk. The helipad was about one hundred yards away.

The weight of the ruck took me back to the first day of basic when a drill sergeant escorted us to our new barracks. They were about a quarter of a mile away, and we walked, carrying our duffel bags. The first hundred yards wasn't hard, but by then some were dragging their bags, and the drill sergeant screamed at them.

"My God! The Lord gave us a bunch of girls this time."

Finally, only about four of us hadn't dropped our bags, so they walked along beside us yelling in our faces.

"If you drop that bag, shithead, I'm going to remember your name for eight full weeks."

During the last hundred yards, I was the only one who hadn't dropped his bag, and I had a sergeant on each side of me, accusing me of being better than everyone else.

"No, Sergeant, I'm not."

"Why haven't you dropped yours yet?" I started to drop it and he yelled, "Don't let it touch the ground!" So I hastily picked it back up and finished the quarter-mile. When he said I could drop it, I did.

"Are you a farm boy?" he asked.

"Yow!" I answered with one of the words not used in the military and ended the scene with fifty push-ups.

When I reached the helipad, I found Sergeant Cuevas, which was good because I sure didn't recognize any of the platoon members. Mike Daugherty came up and said good morning and told me the radio was working. I then asked to be introduced to the platoon.

It was still pretty dark at 0500, so I really didn't get to see too many faces. The first person I met was our medic, Doc Wilson, Elizabethtown, Tennessee. Next was Sergeant Broussard, Raines, Louisiana, the only E-5 (lowest-ranking sergeant) in the platoon. I met each man, a total of thirty-five, counting myself and Sergeant Cuevas.

Only five men can get inside a Huey helicopter with full combat gear, so I grabbed Doc Wilson, Mike Daugherty, Jeffries (one of the machine gunners), and Brent Burford (a rifleman) and headed for the first bird. Then the rest broke into five-man teams, and we were ready to load up.

By then it was 0545, and the sun was beginning to come up, and I saw a sight that I can still remember very vividly today: three hundred men in full combat gear, all locked and loaded, ready to board helicopters. Then sixty Hueys, or slicks as they were so often called, descended in formation, and I realized that my welcome to the war was over. I was there, no mistake. No more questions, no more simulated missions, no more errors; the real thing was upon me, and I still didn't know a half dozen of the names of the men I was responsible for.

"Lord, help me through this first day, and keep my men and me safe," I whispered under the beat of the chopper blades.

Since I was to guard the CP, my bird would land first and secure whatever territory for the captain and the mortar platoon. Edwards sent word that if it was a hot LZ (landing zone), to pop a read smoke immediately so everyone else would know. I knew for sure I was no longer playing games, and I passed the word along to the platoon.

We boarded the open choppers; I was in the middle with two guys facing out on either side of me, and away we went.

3

It was about a thirty-minute ride, and I thought of a thousand things in that half hour: My wife and kids, my family, all the things I hadn't said or done, flashed before me just as clear as could be.

I suppose I was as white as a sheet because everyone else was. I was in the middle. The guys flanking me had their legs dangling in the open air and were holding on to the side of the bird for dear life. It was a one-handed operation because the other hand held an M-16. Although we were relatively safe, I had not experienced an open chopper ride in a combat situation, and when the slick banked sharply, it was harrowing to see the ground spinning by.

"Should I start the ground firing?" Jeffries, our machine gunner, yelled at me.

"Only if you see the enemy or if you're being fired at," I said. "Otherwise, save the sixty for firepower later. We might need it."

My thoughts turned to our helplessness while sitting in an open bird. A ten-year-old squirrel hunter back home with a .22 rifle could have picked off everyone sitting in that Huey, and there was nothing we could have done about it.

My mind shifted to our mission and what infantry really meant in the course of the war. A giddy feeling of pride came over me. On the ground, step for step, soldier for soldier, we were as good as any unit in the world. The whole damned war was centered around the good old American grunt. But first we had to get to the ground. My thoughts whirled.

I felt the chopper start down and I grabbed yellow and red

smoke grenades. The pilot gave a signal, and the two door gunners began firing their M-60 machine guns. I didn't know they
were going to do that, so I thought it meant a hot LZ. I grabbed
my red smoke in one hand and my M-16 in the other. When we
landed, we had about three seconds to unload, then the bird
was gone. In fact, they didn't quite set down. We were about
five feet off the ground.

If you want to know what I felt, put one hundred pounds
on your back and drive down a road about five to ten miles per
hour, then jump out, and you might understand the feeling I
had when that rucksack drove my nose into the ground that
day. The noise of the chopper was so loud that hand signals
were all we could use. We had landed in tall elephant grass,
about twenty yards from the top of the hill.

"I'm hit, I'm hit!" somebody yelled, so I popped a red
smoke, I crawled over to the man. Doc Wilson was already
there, white as a sheet.

"It's a head wound," he shouted.

"I can't tell if we're being shot at," I returned.

Another bird landed, and suddenly I realized how crowded
that small area was, so I told Doc to get the man on the next
chopper before it left. I took the rest of the men to the top of the
hill and formed a perimeter of defense. As we got away from
the choppers where I could hear better, there was no rifle fire,
so I popped a yellow smoke, I broke radio silence and told the
colonel there was one casualty, but we had secured the hilltop.

In a short ten minutes my platoon, the CP, and the mortar
platoon were all on top of what was supposed to be Hill 887.
The captain asked me what had happened, and I told him that
one of my men was yelling that he'd been shot and was bleed-
ing from the left ear, and it looked bad.

"Where's the enemy firing from?" Captain Edwards asked.

"Who knows?" I responded. "I never heard a shot."

Then Mike Daugherty explained that the man had not been
shot but had fallen into the elephant grass, which was razor-

sharp. One blade had punctured his ear, cutting it badly, but he would be fine. I felt relieved, but kind of sheepish.

We started digging in. My platoon and the mortar platoon made a circle around the CP, which consisted of the captain, three radios, Lieutenant Powers, our FO (forward observer), and the medic.

I sat down with the captain and Lieutenant Powers.

"We are here on the map as Hill 887," Captain Edwards began. "Tonight I want you to go on an ambush approximately one hundred meters to the west. Just take a squad with you ... and send your RTO to the CP. I need him. You'll have to break in another one."

I unfolded my map and marked our position, then headed back to my own little CP. Daugherty recommended Kenny Irons from Rhode Island to take his place. Irons wasn't very happy about the idea, but I told him that someone had to do it and that he looked capable to me.

Mike showed us both how to use the "spinning wheel" to code and uncode messages. It was basically very simple. We used a different sheet each day, so our code changed every day. Everyone in the battalion had the same code, as long as the enemy didn't get the wheel. If one got lost, it was reported, and everyone got a new one. I'm not sure how effective it was, but I do know it was a pain in the ass for supply orders.

Doc Melson from Texas was the CP medic, and he was visiting with Doc Wilson. They were easy to get to know, and I felt immediately comfortable with both of them. They explained the malaria pills to me. I told Doc Wilson to be sure that each man took his pills while he was watching.

Kenny Irons and I talked for a long time while digging our foxhole. He was from Smithfield, Rhode Island. I liked Kenny immediately and knew that I could trust him. I tried to learn all I could about his experience in Vietnam and as much as he would share with me about the men.

He showed me a picture of his family and another of himself, prior to being drafted. He had hair almost to his waist in that picture.

"I wasn't growing it in protest," he said, laughing. "It just seemed like the thing to do."

I'd been raised in the fifties when duck tails and crew cuts were the style. I thought that anyone who grew his hair long and had a beard was in Canada. So I put aside another of my small-town prejudices and decided from then on that I'd judge a man by his actions and not by his looks.

Kenny was a typical draftee. He didn't want to be there, but he was doing his duty before going home to the world. Kenny tried to give the impression that he wasn't that good at anything, but anyone with common sense could have seen that he would do what had to be done, and he'd do it well. I knew that if half the men were as good as Kenny, then I'd have no problem.

I ate a C-ration dinner with Lieutenant Powers, who was a college graduate, ROTC, and I was impressed with him, so added another friend to my list. I spent the rest of the afternoon visiting the different positions and talking to the men about fields-of-fire where each position covered a V from its fox-hole out so that we would have every inch covered in a fire fight and discussing what to do in case of attack. I was surprised to find that almost all of them were cherries, as far as contact was concerned, so it would be a learning experience for most of us.

The only E-5 sergeant in the platoon was Adam Broussard, a black man from Raines, Louisiana. I had four blacks assigned to me, but only Adam was in the field. The others were sick or had immersion foot. I liked Adam immediately; however, I wasn't sure how good a leader he was going to be. But I could see he was a good man, and he was willing to try. He'd been in-country for a while.

I told him about the night ambush.

"How many men do you want?" he asked.

"About five good men besides myself and my RTO," I answered.

"Take Poncho, Burford, Stacy, Davis, and Kotewa," he said, naming five men that I didn't know.

I found Jesus "Poncho" Garcia on the list I'd made of all the men in my platoon.

"At 1800 hours, get Burford, Stacy, Davis, and Kotewa together," I said to Poncho. "We're going on an ambush."

"How many mechanical ambushes do you want?" he asked me.

"What the hell is a mechanical ambush?" I asked in return.

He explained that it was a Claymore mine attached to an electrical wire.

"You take two plastic spoons and tie one wire to each spoon. ... You drill a hole in the dish of the spoon," Poncho said. "Then you tie the spoons together and set the Claymore facing the ambush site ... stream, trail, whatever. String a trip wire across the trail, and tie a plastic knife on the end of the trip wire ... and place the knife between the spoons to keep those wires apart. You got about seventy-five feet of wire left which you string back to your position. This is attached to a six-volt battery. Anything that trips the wire sets off the mine."

"Who thought this one up?" I queried.

"I don't know, but it's sure effective. The only way to disarm one is to unhook the wires from the battery."

I liked the idea and told him to bring one along. Then I called the ambush squad together at about 1600 hours. We sat down and talked awhile about home and Vietnam, and then I laid out the plan for the ambush. They all agreed it sounded good.

"If you don't like something, tell me straight out," I said, wanting to be sure they were in favor of every step I was making. "Just because I have had a lot of training sure doesn't make me right. So if you see something you don't like, tell me, so we can all work together."

"Why did you ask me to be on this ambush?" Floyd Kotewa asked.

"Well, you were recommended," I answered.

"I will get him tonight," he responded to nobody in particular.

Somehow I didn't feel that Kotewa meant what he said, but I cautioned myself to remember that remark. Irons told me later, over supper, that Kotewa was a good Joe, but he was always saying, "I'll do it, but I will get you tonight." I felt a little better, but I still stored it in my memory bank until I could know Kotewa better.

At 1800 hours, the seven of us started over the hill, which dropped straight down about twenty feet. It was really hot, and I was glad we had left our rucks on top of the hill. After nearly two hundred feet of steep hill, we hit a large creek of solid rock about forty feet across. I stopped the men and looked at my map. There was no creek that size anywhere near Hill 887. I called Captain Edwards and asked if he was sure we were on Hill 887.

"There is a large creek at the bottom of the hill that doesn't show on my map," I told him.

He reminded me how new I was, and that he knew exactly where we were, and told me not to break radio silence while on ambush patrol. I made the mistake of believing him since he was a captain with experience.

We moved about one hundred meters and found a small animal trail leading to the creek. There was no sign of human activity anywhere, so I decided to use the site for our ambush. Poncho set up his mechanical and I watched him closely. Then we hid in the rocks until full darkness and waited.

For the two hours that followed, I had time to think about all my training and what might or might not be expected of me. One thing I knew for sure was that my decision to become an officer looked like a very poor one.

I had no desire to become an officer back then, nor did I

want to be one now. I made the decision to go to OCS because of financial reasons. I had to sell everything on my small farm when I was drafted because of my divorce, and the day I entered the service I still owed seven thousand dollars and I owned nothing.

My first paycheck as a private had been eighty dollars for a month. Beer and cigarettes took all of it. When I entered OCS, I got the same pay as an E-5 sergeant, which was about $450 per month. Upon graduation, a second lieutenant received seven hundred dollars per month or more.

At the time, it looked like the best way to pay my debts, but now it looked as if I might pay with my life. Had I enlisted for two years, I might still have served in Vietnam, but as a private, who, by now, would have been home coon hunting with his new father-in-law.

Whenever I used to get frustrated, my dad always said, "Son, quit your bitchin' and do something about it." So I began to think positively about my situation. I was reasonably comfortable with the men in the platoon. More people made it home than didn't—and I was, at least, an average person—so the law of averages was on my side.

But the casualty list average wasn't good enough to suit me. I had decided that if I was wounded below the waist in the privates or left a cripple, I would take my life somehow. It might not have been rational thinking, but there was some comfort knowing I was partially in control of my destiny.

I made a pact with God that if I survived in one piece I would be forever grateful. My upbringing had taught me to do what I could in the best way I could and to remember that in the end, God would take care of me as long as I used the gifts he had given me.

For a full two and a half weeks I had been totally alone with nobody to turn to. They were all strangers, and I did not confide easily with just anyone. Being a lieutenant, it was hard to say that I felt inadequate in handling the responsibility bestowed upon me. But the positive thoughts began rolling in again. At least there was a semblance of home now. There would be the same faces every day, with the chance to make friends and hopefully find one to confide in.

My thoughts turned back to the mission. I knew that some-time during the night, Lieutenant Powers, under the direction of Captain Edwards, would be firing artillery. The "arty" units would establish our position by firing 105mm rounds about one thousand meters away; north gun one, east gun two, south gun three and west gun four. The object, of course, was to pro-vide instant assistance if we got into enemy contact. It was very effective and something I would use a lot in the months that followed.

The first thing they fired was a smoke bomb during the day, then white phosphorous at night as a marking round. If a platoon was where it should have been, then the Willie Pete (white phosphorous) went off about one thousand meters to its north and up in the sky.

I had no more than thought of that when that Willie Pete went off, and I swore it was directly over my head. I broke radio silence for the second time and told Edwards about it, and he said it just seemed like it went off overhead, that my judgment of distance at night was way off.

"Don't break radio silence again unless it's an emergency," he ordered.

Well, after a person confirmed that Willie Pete was cor-rect, he got the real thing, and I don't mean Coca-Cola. The first HE (high explosive) went off about one hundred meters away, and shrapnel flew through the trees everywhere. Luckily for us, we were down in the creek bed. Then several rounds went off really close by. I grabbed the radio and broke silence for the third time.

Now, I came from a long line of preachers, teachers, and cussers, and there is a time for all three methods to be used, but I chose the later and yelled into the radio:

"Cease fire, you motherfuckers! Cease fire!"

Things got quiet in a hurry. Captain Edwards called me and told us to come back at first light as we were not where he thought we were. I thought, No shit, Sherlock! He also said he would talk to me about radio procedure the next day.

There I was, my first platoon, my first night, my first ambush; it was so hot I could hardly breathe, so dark I couldn't see my hand in front of me. The solid rock was biting into my butt; I almost got killed by friendly fire, and the captain wanted to talk about radio procedure.

After about an hour, fatigue overcame us, and we tried to take turns resting. Kotewa told me to bring my two-quart canteen to use as a pillow, and I thought it sounded crazy, but I saw everyone else using theirs.

I lay down in the solid rock to try to rest. You ought to try it sometime, especially in the dark. I placed the canteen down, and my head was the only comfortable part of my body. It felt like Indians had secured a thousand arrowheads straight up in the ground. It was difficult to be quiet, and I heard Kotewa say just before I dozed off, "I will get you tonight."

I'd just gotten to sleep when something hit me in the face. I jumped up like a scared rabbit and hissed, "What was that?" No one answered so I thought they were messing with the new guy, and I lay back down. This happened about four or five times during the night, and I was getting a little perturbed, but there was nothing I could do.

I took my turn at watch about 0400 since most trouble happened at dawn. Daylight came, and all was quiet. I can still see Kenny Irons sound asleep in the rocks. How, I'll never know, but some people can sleep anywhere. We woke everyone up as soon as we could see clearly.

When I picked up my canteen, a little kangaroo rat jumped into his den, and I started laughing out loud. When I told everyone what had happened, including my suspicions, they joined in the laughter. I wasn't too fond of rats anyway, so from that day on I could hear a spider making its web if it was close to my sleeping area. I wish it had been the men playing with the new guy instead of a rat.

We started humping back to the CP, and all went well until we reached the drop-off. It was straight up, and we had to use both hands to keep from falling. It took thirty minutes to climb that last twenty feet. I met Lieutenant Powers at the top and he told me the captain wanted to see me in about fifteen minutes. Powers said he thought the captain finally knew where we were.

"It won't take long to figure it out," I said. I put my map down and showed him where I thought we were.

"You may be right," he said, "but the CO thinks we're on Hill 820."

"I'm sure we're on 830," I replied. I explained that if the one-oh-five rounds were supposed to go off one thousand meters to the north of Hill 887, and they landed on top of my men, which was only one hundred meters from where we were standing, then nineteen hundred meters to the south would establish a line, and Hill 830 was the only hill on that line.

Powers finally agreed with me, but said the captain was positive about Hill 820.

Right then, a slick flew over, so I called him on the radio and asked for a grid location. I learned another valuable lesson. We grunts had to shackle everything in code, but pilots used plain English. He gave the exact grid location of Hill 830. My fifteen-minute wait to see Captain Edwards came early when he heard my transmission with the pilot. He came over stalking mad.

"I hope you're happy," he spat out the words. "Now the entire NVA (North Vietnamese Army) knows our location."

Kotewa walked by then and said, "Captain, I will get you tonight."

The CO was furious. I apologized for my misconduct, but my newfound knowledge was very helpful. I was learning quickly.

The colonel called and spoke in plain English, "Choppers on the way to airlift you off Hill 830 and over to Hill 887. Landing time, ten minutes."

I was forgotten as everyone scrambled to pack for the move. Since I hadn't unpacked the night before, I used the next ten minutes to study my map so I'd know where I was. The maps we used were topographical in that they gave elevation lines. Each little brown line represented twenty feet of elevation, and only the hilltops were given a number. I wouldn't need anyone to point out our location after that. It's one reason I'm here today.

We landed on 887 and all was quiet. We dug in, and again Sergeant Cuevas and I set up our fields-of-fire. Hill 887 was a good deal larger than 830, so we spread out farther. Our objective was to support First and Third Platoons as they would be on reconnaissance in force. Actually, they were no more than a quarter-mile from us, most of the time, but about one mile on foot. They were on the next ridgeline, 440 yards as the crow flies.

Our mortar platoon was set up and would fire a few rounds to keep location and direction so that they had support if they needed it. I began to see why Lieutenant Cross, whom I'd only met briefly, had told me to know where I was at all times or our own men would blow us away.

As First and Third Platoons moved, they would continually give situation reports, tell us what they had found, and mention other pertinent information. As I sat on Hill 887, I felt good about the platoon and the short recons that we'd been on.

Each day, one squad would leave the perimeter, go a short distance, and then return. Each night, we set out listening posts. No one reported any sign of the enemy. First and Third reported no trail or signs. My reaction was one of joy.

I was gaining valuable time to observe the real Army in action. We could monitor all the other companies, and, by changing channels, monitor their entire operations. There was heavy fighting in some areas, but none in ours. The only discomfort I had was my growing mistrust for Captain Edwards.

4

A feeling of false security was setting in on me as well as the rest of the men. On the third day, we were re-supplied with beans and bullets. We also gained three new men, Lt. Michael Dalton, Private First Class Palmer, and Private First Class Smith. Again I felt good because I wasn't the newest man anymore. Sergeant Cuevas placed Palmer and Smith in their squads, and Dalton and I visited.

I knew right away that Mike was that close friend I was looking for. We hit it off immediately. The CO told Mike to keep his ruck ready because at any time he would be given a platoon. The Third Platoon lieutenant was due to go home in a week. I told Mike he was lucky because he would have a couple of days to settle in before the other lieutenant left.

The sound of rifle fire from across the ridgeline came like a siren in the night. We all rushed to the hillside to watch and listen on the radio. Lieutenant Cross was wounded, and two men were dead. The jungle was so thick that we could not see people, but we could see the enemy's green tracers and our own red tracers going off everywhere. I had always heard that a person could tell the difference between the Russian AK-47 and the American M-16, and it proved to be very true. When the Russian gun went off, it sounded a loud, but very distinctive popping noise.

We could not help First Platoon, yet we could almost see the men. Apparently, Lieutenant Cross had stopped the platoon for a short break, and as fate would have it, at least three of the enemy were hiding inches away, hoping First Platoon would pass on by. When Lieutenant Cross sat down, his feet were nearly touching one of the enemy. The NVA opened up at point-blank range, killing two men and wounding Lieutenant Cross. Then they ran into the jungle. The fire fight seemed to last forever.

Medevacs came in and got Lieutenant Cross and the dead. When they popped a yellow smoke to notify the others of the position, six other smoke grenades showed up through the jungle. Two were violet, two were yellow, and two were red. The enemy was wise to our procedure.

As soon as the fire fight was over, Colonel Sutton flew to our location in a Bumblebee (Loach helicopter, two-seater). When he landed, the CO told me to ride with the pilot until we were called back, so I jumped in the colonel's seat and we took off like a bat out of hell.

The pilot motioned for me to put on the headset. He asked me what I wanted to see, and I told him I didn't have any idea; I was new in-country and this was my first mission.

"How about a low-level look at the surrounding area and the stream beds?" he asked, and I made a big mistake by nodding my head in agreement.

If you've ever imagined what riding on the back of a real bumblebee would be like, I can tell you. I suppose one had to be a pretty good flier to be a colonel's pilot, and maybe just a little crazy. We didn't miss any treetops by more than three inches, and when it was time to see the creek beds, I thought we'd be part of them.

The pilot handed me a smoke grenade.

"If you see anything, let me know," he said. "You mark the spot with the smoke, and the arty boys can have some fun." Just then, the colonel called us back and not a second too soon. One more dipsy-do-da and my C-ration shit would have become a C-ration upchuck.

The CO called Powers, Dalton, and me to a meeting where we sat down with our maps. Edwards told Mike he would be on a bird to First Platoon in a few minutes and to get his men to an LZ as quickly as possible because we were all moving north to the Rockpile. The fighting was heavy there, and our battalion needed more support.

Our first stop was Ca Lou for a shower, clean clothes, and a hot meal. Mike and I said a temporary goodbye and shook hands. I used the old-movie-mountain-man saying of "Watch your topknot!"

We all rucked up and awaited our freedom birds to take us to hot showers. I was wrong again. In a field unit, there was no such thing as hot water, except in a canteen or helmet.

When we landed in Ca Lou, it was like a beehive. It was a flat area with tanks, APCs (armored personnel carriers), jeeps by the dozens, two-and-a-half–ton trucks, you name it, and it was there and moving.

We took a community shower in water warmed by the sun, got clean clothes, and ate chow in the Mermac cans which were supposed to keep the food hot. I thought they'd cooked it the day before. The carrots were turning green around the edges, but it was a change from C-rations, and I was supposed to be thankful.

Colonel Sutton called a briefing where I met Lieutenant Dalton once again, as well as a brand new butter-bar by the name of Johnson. It was only ten days into the mission at this point, and Captain Edwards announced that I was his senior lieutenant. I'd heard of moving up fast, but that seemed ridiculous.

The colonel told us that a place call Don Kke Sak had been overrun by a regiment of NVA regulars. Firebase Scotch had been overrun, too. Several of our men had been killed and several more had been wounded. Our mission was to land on a hilltop called Nui Bi Lo where fifty people of the 501st Battalion had been killed or wounded only ten days earlier. Our

Charlie Company had relieved them and had one killed and fourteen wounded.

When I asked for more details, I learned that they were being mortared constantly. The enemy attacked them at night and fired 122mm rockets during the day. We were to replace Charlie Company and then walk down the ridgeline back to the flat. We were told to search-and-destroy anything we could. Departure time was 0900 the following day.

The colonel told us that there were three missing bodies that no one had picked up. If we found them, we were to send them in a chopper. They had been missing for at least three days, and it was possible that the enemy had them. The few survivors had reported them dead or wounded, but could not help them.

The thought of leaving American bodies on foreign soil was something new to me. I knew I'd want to be buried in Casey, Illinois, if I had the choice. If at all possible, my platoon would find them and send them home. They probably wouldn't be too hard to find after three or four days in the heat.

Dalton and I went off to the side of one tent and talked for a while. It looked like all hell was going to break loose for us the next day. Mike told me that his wife was due to a have a baby in March. He was really scared for his platoon and his family.

He was expressing the type of thoughts that I hadn't been able to discuss until then. His sense of duty had brought him to Vietnam. Patriotism was glowing all around him, but the reality of death and the heavy burden of being a lieutenant were causing him to doubt his ability. I felt the same way.

I expressed my thoughts about Captain Edwards' inability to lead a grunt company, and Mike told me he'd sensed the same problem. We agreed then that we'd make our own decisions regarding every move we made. If need be, we'd talk directly to each other over the radio and support each other at all times.

We both knew we had good men whom we could trust, but we also knew that our fears could not be relayed to them.

I can't describe the comradeship that was formed then. At that point I would have died for Mike, and I knew he would have done the same for me. We built a closeness in those few, short minutes that most men never achieve in a lifetime.

I returned to the platoon and told everyone to get a good night's rest because in the early morning it would be back to the boondocks. It was then that I noticed a fresh pack of Marlboro cigarettes, and I asked where it came from. Up until then I only had C-rations cigarettes, and Marlboro, my favorite brand, looked like a true friend.

Kenny Irons told me there was a PX (Army store) over by the mess hall.

"Better hurry or you won't have much choice," he added.

I beat it over there and found a semi-trailer with a door on the side and another on the end. I walked in and was surprised to see a small grocery store. If a person wanted to shave or take a bath, there was plenty of soap and razors.

All the good magazines were gone; only a few off-brand girlie books remained. And there were only Kent, Lucky, Camel, and Pall Mall cigarettes left, so I bought a carton of Kents, which was my last choice before non-filtered smokes.

The sergeant in charge was smoking a Marlboro and reading a Playboy, so I jumped him about the lack of good smokes and magazines. He told me they were sold out. Now I never really wanted to be an officer in the beginning, and probably only used the authority to the point of being called a lifer about three times in my short career, but I demanded to know where he got his fags and mags. He just grinned.

That set off the time bomb. I asked him how many he had, and the grin left his face. We marched up to the truck cab. Now I never threatened this man at all, but I was carrying my M-16 out of habit. I casually mentioned that Marlboros were my favorite, and I would deem it an honor if he sold me a few. When he opened the sleeper compartment, there were about twenty cartons of Marlboros and several Playboys.

"They are for officers above the rank of major," he said sheepishly.

"I'll take four cartons and four Playboys at regular price," I told him. I'd been sending all my money home except for a hundred dollars a month, but I wanted a little bit of luxury when it was available.

He crawled into the sleeper and started moving things around, and I spotted several cases of Pepsi. I'd been a Pepsiholic since the age of thirteen, so I asked for a case of soda as well.

"No way. These are private stock. Spoken for by a colonel," he exclaimed. There must have been a dozen cases, and I was going to the field the next day, so I grabbed a case and paid him ten dollars extra.

"If the higher-ranking officers miss this stuff, tell them to come see me and I'll be glad to share," I remarked as I left. I was almost out of earshot when I heard him mutter, "Damn grunts. Think they own this war."

If we don't, we damn well should, I thought.

I ran into Colonel Sutton, whom I had learned to respect very highly. I was still hot under the collar, and I told him what had happened. I told him I'd paid for mine and would be willing to chip in for the rest.

When we entered the PX and the sergeant saw me, I was sure he could have killed me on sight, but I really didn't care. He told the colonel I had threatened him, so I rehashed all my moves with the M-16, and the colonel saw no threat.

We went to the cab of the truck and unloaded everything that was supposed to be in the PX. There was about five hundred dollars worth of stuff, according to the sergeant. Colonel Sutton paid him in full and told him to keep his mouth shut and no report would be written.

We took all the goods to the colonel's hootch, and he assured us it would be sold to the Third, 187th, at cost, and to no one else. We put the word out, and it wasn't long before the colonel got his money back.

I held a briefing the next morning and told the platoon our mission. Dennis Davis and Tex Lissenbee were the two main point-men for the platoon, although Loughan, Rosencranse, and a few others had all worked the position.

We were assigned a Kansas City Star, which was a VC (Viet Cong) or NVA prisoner, who, after a few weeks training, had the choice of walking point for American patrols instead of going to prison. His name was Tang, and Dennis Davis got along pretty well with him, so they buddied up as a point-team. The two machine gunners were Jeffries and Tyler, both capable men. We talked about their MG jobs: when to use one and how to save ammunition. The purpose of an M-60 was to have a large amount of firepower in cases of being overrun. It was not to be used except in an emergency.

The rest of the men were either riflemen or grenadiers. Everyone had a specific job and carried extra ammo for the sixty or batteries for the radios. We had three fire teams or squads, each with about eleven men. Each squad had a point team and a radio team. We were as ready as we could be for Nui Bi Lo.

5

The next morning our platoon was airlifted first. When we landed, 122mm rockets greeted us from all around the hilltop. It was far too small a place for a whole company of about one hundred fifty men.

As we got off the birds, Charlie Company got on. We could tell they were tired. They had seen the Elephant. I don't know where the expression comes form, but it means "seen the worst."

We had incoming rounds all day long, but somehow we managed the changeover without a casualty. Several birds took small-arms fire, but there were no losses.

I found it hard to believe that there wasn't a single casualty in the exchange. I spent more time on my belly that day doing the low-crawl that all basic trainees were taught. I realized that as much as I had hated it in training, I was glad I'd learned how to stay down.

Everyone was crowded. I couldn't believe they expected us to survive on such a small hilltop. My old drill sergeant used to tell us to spread out or one small Ping-Pong ball would wipe us all out. He should have seen us then. But we didn't have a choice because the lifers had put us there.

At 1600 hours, I told the captain that it was too crowded on the hill and that I'd like to take my platoon a short distance down a narrow finger to set up an ambush and listening post for the company. He agreed, and we started down a narrow trail. About one hundred meters ahead of me, Tang and Davis stopped. I went forward to check it out.

It was the scene of a previous ambush, only it was the Americans who had been surprised. There were articles of clothing, helmets, and blood on the undergrowth. Charlie Kress picked up a helmet.

"No one touches anything of the dead," I said, and several men agreed.

I called the CO to report and asked if the three bodies were supposed to be in the area. I was told that Charlie Company had found them and had bagged up what was left to send home. The smell of death told me all I needed to know. We moved on about another hundred meters, and the finger dropped off; we could go no further. We dug in as best we could, for it was getting late, and after dark it was impossible to see.

At about 2100 hours, I had the artillery boys fire my NDP (nighttime defensive position). I walked the shells a little closer than usual because I was a little scared, and it made me feel good to know they were ready to support us if we needed it.

At 2200 hours, the artillery started again, and it was getting closer. I asked them to stop and they told me they weren't firing. The enemy was after us again.

They continued throughout the night, and I understood why Charlie Company had looked so ragged. There was no way a person could sleep or rest. I knew I wasn't going to stay on that hill while the men were picked off by artillery fire.

We returned to the command post the next morning. I requested to leave the hill for reconnaissance and to search-and-destroy as ordered. The CO said that was fine, but he wanted us to leave after 1200 hours. He was planning some type of strategy for the three platoons. He decided I should leave in a northerly direction toward the Rockpile, which we could see from the top of Nui Bi Lo. The cave openings were visible to the naked eye.

We would be leaving the hill on a ridgeline called the Razorback. First Platoon would be about one hour behind us; if we had any trouble, they would be close for support. Lieutenant Johnson and the mortar platoon would stay put for a while. If it was safe, they would follow the next day.

We rucked up at about 1300 hours and started down the ridgeline. I was glad to leave Purple Heart Ridge. There must have been a Purple Heart Ridge in every war. We felt that Nui Bi Lo deserved the name because, in thirteen days, there had been sixty-four casualties and no enemy killed that we could prove.

For the next three days, we took every step carefully and everyone was alert. It was terribly hot and humid, but we trudged on. My secret objective was the flats, which were only about four klicks (kilometers) away. I knew that the Fifth Mechanized Unit was there in heavy concentration. I didn't tell anyone but Mike what the strategy was. It was very plain that we were in enemy territory, and we couldn't fight them success-fully. I felt like I was walking right through their living room.

On the third day, we set up for chow about noon. The colonel called and told us to cut an LZ because the command post and mortar platoon were catching up with us. We were in a good location for the airlift, and they all flew in, so once again we were company-sized. Lieutenant Johnson got to ride in the colonel's Bumblebee. They had no more than left when we received incoming rounds from 82mm mortars.

Charlie Kress hollered for me to come over to line posi-tion, so I ran over to see what was up. We could hear the dinks firing the mortar on the next ridgeline. Several rounds were being fired at us from at least two different tubes, and they were getting close. One or two rounds landed inside the perim-eter. The blast threw rocks all over me, and I felt blood on one of my fingers. I yelled for Jeffries and his M-60.

He set up quickly and I told him to fire as soon as he heard the tube pop. Three or four of us opened up with Jeffries, and that was the end of the mortaring. We had no idea whether we hit anything or not, but I was sure we had to have been close because we saw the puff of smoke come out of the tube, and we must have put a thousand rounds within a thirty-foot circle of it. We might have killed a few men, but there was no way to know except to check out the area, and it was too late in the day for a long recon. If we didn't get them, they would be back that night, and I didn't feel like hanging around.

The colonel left and we started to pack for a quick move. We backtracked about one hundred meters and then went down-hill. At the bottom, Charlie Kress found a trail and stopped us. I went forward and my stomach turned over about halfway. It was not only a trail, but a heavily traveled foot path. At home, when the old cows followed the same route everyday, they made a path about twelve inches wide and about two inches deep

The trail had been cut through the underbrush so it couldn't be seen from the air. It was almost three feet wide and five feet high. For the Vietnamese, it was a thoroughfare, but we had to stoop over just to get through. Then we caught our rucks on vines and bushes.

The scary part was the communications wire that ran along the trail. If the enemy concentration was heavy enough to have communications, then there had to be at least a battalion-sized element, which meant we were outnumbered five to one.

I reported to the captain and he told us to get the hell up the hill and dig in. I left four men to watch the trail so the company could pass through, then I went about two hundred meters and found an area that we could use for an NDP. With a little work, birds could land, and there was a lot of security in that knowledge.

Halfway up the hill, Captain Edwards passed out from the heat, so that slowed us down a little, but by four o'clock, our perimeter was set up, the LZ cut, and everyone was digging in. We backtracked to the thoroughfare and set up a mechanical ambush, knowing we could kill a half dozen dinks and wound a few more. Since it was so far from our perimeter, we had to hide the battery about seventy-five feet from the trail. I can't remember whose mechanical it was, but they did a perfect job of setting it up, and we returned to the perimeter.

That night, we set up four more mechanicals and several Claymore mines. There wasn't a doubt that we would be hit, so we prepared as best we could. We kept 100 percent alert all night long. Several times we heard movement from different points of the perimeter. Each time, we either fired a warning shot or blew a Claymore.

At about 3 A.M., one of the mechanicals went off. The CO called it in, and he was told to check it out, so he left me to handle it. I said I would check it out at daylight. We argued for a good while, and finally Lieutenant Johnson said he would go since it was one of his mechanicals.

"Whatever tripped that wire is either dead or wounded," I

told him. "If you leave the perimeter after dark, you're inviting ambush. Your own men might even get you."

But I was ignored. As a result, two men were wounded. I wasn't sure if it was the enemy or our own men who did it. We couldn't get medevacs at night in the hills, so the wounded men had to wait until morning. I was upset with the CO and Johnson both. I knew that Second Platoon hadn't done any shooting, but when it got dark, a man shot at anything that moved or seemed to move.

Dalton and I got together and decided to save all the ammunition we could because we knew it might get rough the next day. We passed the word to conserve, unless the men were sure of an attack.

A medevac came in at daylight and took the wounded out amidst small-arms fire, but we couldn't see where the shots came from. When the chopper left, we checked out all the mechanicals. The one that had gone off had killed a mongoose. That was the biggest fault of the mechanical; it didn't differentiate between man or beast, large or small. Results: two wounded GIs, and one dead enemy mongoose.

When we went after another of our mechanicals, it was gone. All of it was gone. We stopped immediately and backed up a few steps. My stomach turned over. It was a sick feeling for two reasons: The only way to steal a mechanical was to have seen someone set it up, which meant, in the jungle, that the enemy had been within a few feet of us all the time. And secondly, it had probably been set up again to kill us.

We backtracked to the perimeter and I reported to Captain Edwards. He was furious.

"How could that have happened?" he demanded.

"The enemy must be all around us," I answered. "They saw us set them all up. Ours was the only one they could steal because the battery was outside the perimeter. If we can keep from being ambushed with our own mechanical, we'll be lucky. We're lucky to have only two casualties already."

We agreed, for once, on our locations, and called artillery for some H-and-I (harassment and interdiction) fire. They gave us orders to leave the area for better ground and I disagreed. We felt that if we backtracked, we should cut new trail for fear of being ambushed on the old trail.

The only other way was to go downhill and back up where the 82mm had shot at us the day before. Mike and I wanted to cut a new trail toward this area. If they had placed an ambush there, it would be a better choice than booby traps on the old trail.

After considerable disagreement, Dalton, Power, and Johnson, and I finally won out, and Dalton's men took the point platoon while Johnson's brought up the rear. Second Platoon flanked the mortar platoon and command post.

We covered more ground that day, going mainly uphill. When we finally reached the top of the ridgeline we were supposed to be on, we found a good defensive position and set up our perimeter for the night.

The next day was resupply day, so we cut a bigger LZ than usual. Being company size, it took about six birds to resupply us. We had gone nine days without showers, and some of our clothing was ripped off because of "wait-a-minute" vines.

Mike and I had decided we weren't carrying enough firepower, so we had ordered extra hand grenades and Claymores, as well as extra ammo for our guns. The amount of hand grenades and Claymores each man carried had been left to the individual's choosing. Some carried none at all; some carried five or more. Mike and I hadn't carried any but were more than willing to start. We asked each man to carry ten hand grenades and one Claymore.

Along with resupply, I received my first mail, and it made me realize how far away home was.

Home was ten thousand miles away, along with all the security that a man grew up with. My older brother had graduated from the Air Force Academy and had already served at least one tour of duty flying B-52 bombers. In fact, our LZ was an old crater that my letters from home ended up in.

I had come to realize that while I feared most for the lives of the men, my family was ten thousand miles away fearing for my safety. I couldn't write home any positive thoughts. My only salvation was in the busy schedule we had. I didn't have any length of time to dwell on anything except survival.

After our hot meal of roast beef and carrots, we all had some free time. Usually, on resupply day we didn't have time to do much of anything. We took turns pulling perimeter guard and wrote a few lines home, repaired equipment, and cleaned weapons.

Resupply came on every third day, and I always looked forward to it because we came in contact with the real world, via the mail pouch. If I didn't receive mail, someone always did, and was glad to read aloud or share even the most intimate letter. It was also a day that brought a little rest and recuperation. We had a chance to think about things and to get to know everyone a little better.

I wrote home to ask for four things that day: a case of Pepsi, Marlboro cigarettes, orange Kool-Aid, and a pair of leather gloves. I never gave a thought about the cost of sending a care package that size. I figured if I was going to die, I wanted one last Marlboro and one last Pepsi. The water we drank had to have iodine tablets, which ruined the taste, but orange Kool-Aid brought the taste back to a tolerable level. The gloves were for the briars and bamboo. I thought that life would be a whole lot better if I had those four things to sustain me.

Mike and I got to know each other much better, and then I spent some time with the rest of the men. I had only been with them two weeks, but I was learning quickly. The command post medic, Doc Melson and Tex Lissenbee, one of the point men, were both from Texas. These two and Doc Wilson were always together. Doc Melson had a line of bullshit that could keep anyone occupied for days.

Jim Stacy was from Massachusetts, and I knew from our first meeting that his head was on right and he had a good attitude. There were three Mexican-Americans: Angel Ruiz, Poncho Garcia, and Sandoval. Sergeant Cuevas was Puerto Rican, and besides Sergeant Broussard, there were three other blacks: James, Tyler, and Mosely.

They came from all over the United States from all sorts of backgrounds. The only missing group was the upper-middle-class rich boys, at least in the draftees' rank. Out of the whole platoon, there were only two men I didn't trust, and they were no threat except that I couldn't count on them to do anything right, and I couldn't believe anything they told me. Out of about thirty-five men, I couldn't have asked for an overall better bunch of eighteen-year-olds.

I took the opportunity to sit down with Floyd Kotewa. His first words were, "I ain't gonna do it, and I will get you tonight."

"Better do it right or I will get you tomorrow night," I replied.

"I got your tomorrow night right here," he answered. And he grabbed his pecker.

I think Floyd was from Detroit, and I asked him what he was doing in the service. He told me that he had to choose between a penal farm or Vietnam. After he explained what he had done, I knew he only lived to go home for revenge.

At seventeen, he said he'd been caught stealing two candy bars. The store manager prosecuted for shoplifting. It had really made Floyd mad, so he went back and stole again. His idea was not only to steal more, but also to show the store manager that he could get him. Well, he got caught again, so they gave him his choice.

I asked him what he was going to do when he got out of the service, and he said he was going back to burn the store to the ground. I wasn't really sure if he meant what he said, but I told him if he just did his job, we would get along fine.

"I got your job right here!" was his final comment. And he grabbed his pecker again. Despite Floyd's way of acting, everyone liked and respected him. We enjoyed his little side antics.

One of the essentials of a grunt platoon was a deck of cards, and everyone had at least one deck. A game called Spades was about all we played in the field. Anytime we had a five-minute break, someone would deal. Score was kept on everything, and every game was completed, even if it took days. If somebody had to pull guard or go on patrol, the card game would stop and someone would say, "Man, don't you get killed 'cause I got one helluva hand." Some guys would carry their hands with them and finish the game the first chance they got. Poncho usually carried four or five decks and sometimes had as many games going.

I visited all afternoon and then got ready for total darkness. The evening was uneventful, except for a few humorous activities.

About midnight, someone in the next position started whispering, "Medic, medic."

Doc Wilson grabbed his medical bag and went the fifteen feet. He asked what the trouble was.

A voice said, "Doc, I got a hard-on. Would you relieve it for me?"

Old Doc was a slow-draw Tennessee, and he came back hopping mad.

6

The Ghenko lizard was a small reptile that fed at night. It was basically harmless, but it had a nighttime call that caused a lot of hard feelings between lifers and draftees. Its sound was a loud and distinct, "Puck you-u-u." Sometimes it would go. "Puck, puck, puck you-u-u." Naturally, the American GI didn't speak the local lizard language and interpreted it as "Fuck you."

The men thought they'd have some fun. They weren't happy with the CO because of his map reading and his passing out. Someone would holler, "Captain Edwards!"

"What?" he'd answer.

"Fuck you!" the voice would return.

Edwards couldn't take it.

I went back to my position and spoke to the men. "Guys," I tried, "the CO doesn't think it's funny, and he wants it stopped." Porky was the CO's nickname, and apparently he knew it because he called me back again. He told me that if they didn't quit, we would be point platoon forever. I told the guys to knock it off, and they did, for a few minutes.

After my fifth trip over to the CO, I tried to reason with him. I told him I couldn't tell who was doing it in the dark, but he would have none of it.

I was getting tired, and it was my turn to sleep for a while. I walked back to my position, but on the way I tripped and fell down. In a very clear and recognizable voice I called out, "Captain Edwards!"

"What?"

"Fuck you, fuck you!" I answered sarcastically, still face down on the ground.

The next morning, at dawn, several men were hollering,

"Doc, Doc!"

"I don't make house calls," he answered dryly.

The captain hadn't gotten much sleep. I told him he was taking everything too seriously, but he was like Floyd. He wouldn't listen. Second Platoon saddled up to be lead platoon when it would have been First or Third Platoon's turn. Several of the men grabbed their peckers and chimed, "We got his point platoon right here!" Floyd was well liked. I never worried about his intentions after that.

Tex Lissenbee was the point-man that day. We covered about three hundred meters and set up again, but the command post stayed behind. We were only a few hundred meters apart, but in the jungle it was like a thousand miles, especially when darkness came.

We all had our personal fears, but basically we all thought alike when it came to fields-of-fire at night. We checked out every tree so that if a hand grenade were thrown, it wouldn't bounce back on top of us. The killing radius of a hand grenade was thirty-five meters, so it helped to know where a man was going to throw it.

Every rock would be located. Every possible avenue of approach would be covered by either a Claymore, a mechanical, or an M-60. If time permitted, fields-of-fire were cut with machetes.

All this took place before dark. As darkness settled in, we were confident of everything in front of us. Each position was a four-man position. Only one man stayed awake, unless otherwise ordered.

I remember an incident with Angel Ruiz. He seldom pulled bunker guard without seeing or hearing something. On this occasion he'd cut down a banana tree about thirty feet in front of his position. The stub of the tree was about two feet high. Around midnight, he radioed enemy movement. I told him to wake up his three bunkermates to see if they could hear or see the movement.

"There's still movement to my front," Ruiz reported about fifteen minutes later.

I crawled over to his position, and watched and listened for an hour and a half. He kept trying to convince me that the banana tree was moving. I assured him that it wasn't. I told him not to fire without being sure of himself, then I crawled back to my position and waited.

At 4 A.M., Angel was on guard again. Once more he called in enemy movement. I crawled back over to him.

"Angel, none of your friends saw any movement. That banana tree hasn't moved."

"Maybe. But there are two objects out there now," he insisted.

We sat and watched for an hour until I began to see movement myself. It was getting to be daylight so we woke everybody up for 100 percent alert. Nothing happened. Angel and I went out to the banana tree.

I was about to give him a father-to-son talk because it wasn't the first time he'd kept me awake for no reason. Then I hit the dirt. There, by the banana tree, were two sets of knee and elbow prints. We tracked the two men to three different locations around our perimeter. If Angel, or any other man pulling bunker guard had been asleep, we probably would have been attacked. Angel was wrong nine times out of ten, but I realized that an alert, scared GI was better than one who went to sleep unconcerned.

In the morning, we went on patrol to scout the area. We started down the west side of the ridgeline. Dennis Davis was first in line, then Tang, a rifleman, myself, and Kenny Irons noticed an abundance of flies a few feet to our left front. We slowly approached the flies, and the smell was terrible. We couldn't figure it out until Davis moved a couple of rocks, exposing human feces.

Security was called immediately, which meant we had to be as silent as possible, and every other man was to face out and fire at anything that moved.

Dennis, Tang, and I looked around and found a total of five shitters. The Vietnamese dug small holes and then slid two slabs of rock together, leaving about a two-inch crack between them. Four of the shitters had been filled and one was fresh. We knew they had to be close by. Everyone was really tense.

Dennis moved on downhill about twenty feet and stopped again. I crawled up to see and he pointed down. I peeked over the edge of a sharp, six-foot drop-off, and what I saw caused my heart to beat faster. A pair of tennis shoes was pointing up as if a person was reclining on his back. We tossed a grenade in the bunker and fell back a few feet.

The platoon spread out, and radio reports said we were stumbling over bunkers. We alerted the CO and he, in turn, alerted the colonel. We checked out the area and found a total of thirty-seven bunkers, well used, with warm rice heating on two different stoves. My orders were to disturb nothing and to return to the top of the hill.

Mike's platoon joined us that evening, and the Third Platoon and CP stayed where they were for mortar support. The CO told us to set up a squad-sized ambush that night, but I had no desire to split our elements and be at the bottom of the hill after dark.

Mike and I discussed the situation and decided that a mechanical would be sufficient, and at first light we would go back down. To this day, I don't suppose anyone but Mike and me knew that a mechanical replaced several men, but at the time, disobeying an order seemed the best alternative. We felt that if some of the men were down below and some on top, and the enemy got between us, we couldn't fire a shot for fear of hitting our own men, and our ambush would be wiped out. We sent a squad back down to set up a mechanical.

Our mission, the next day, was to destroy everything and then move out. As we went back down to retrieve the mechanical, we were all primed and ready. Today's tennis shoes might have feet in them, I thought.

The ambush was intact, just as we had left it. We moved on past the bunker and found a strange-looking setup. It was a semi-underground mess hall. The chimney for cooking passed through four or five stove pipes. The idea was ingenious. Very little smoke came out of the chimney, and by the time it filtered through the jungle, no smoke could be seen from above.

Tang, our scout, had crawled in a hole and disappeared. When he stuck his head out the other end, Simmons pointed his M-16 and fired. The weapon misfired, and that's all that saved Tang's life.

We went a little further and a rock wall caused us to proceed one at a time. Davis and Tang disappeared around the rock, and suddenly Davis opened up. We all hit the dirt and waited. I yelled at Davis and he came back around the rock wall. He said he walked into three dinks at "sling arms." He had wounded at least one before they ran. We moved forward at a snail's pace. There was blood in big globs everywhere. We followed the blood trail to a large rock-bed creek and set up security all around.

Mike sent a squad down to help out. With good security, Davis, Stacy, Irons, and I followed the blood trail. Having been a hunter and tracker back home, I was pretty sure Davis had wounded two. One was not bad, the other appeared to be a serious wound. I elected to follow the worse of the two.

For about two hours, we hunted a wounded animal. Each step was an eternity for me. Every radio transmission sounded like a police siren screaming, "Here we are!" Finally we found where the NVA had stopped and bandaged his wound, and an extra set of footprints showed up. I decided the NVA could only be pushed so hard, and then they would ambush us, so we returned to the bunker complex.

We started a detailed search of the bunkers. In the one where we had blown away the tennis shoes, I found a piece of paper with all thirty-seven bunkers drawn on it. There were arrows pointing across the creek and then circling back up to the top of the hill where Mike was waiting. I called him immediately and told him what I had found. I interpreted the arrows as a counter attack.

About then, the men on the creek opened fire. I ran down to them and they said that they had fired at six dinks who were coming down the creek. They didn't know if they had killed any or not. The jungle was so thick that if a person fell down and kept still, no one would see him. Then Mike's platoon fired at three more dinks coming up the ridgeline. They wounded at least one.

Captain Edwards called, and, from his higher position, saw seven dinks coming down the ridgeline towards Mike. By the end of the day, we had destroyed all the bunkers and had fired upon the enemy several times, but we had no body count. I was sure that if we would have had dogs, we could have found at least three dead or dying, and another half dozen seriously wounded, but the jungle was a dangerous place to track wounded enemy. We were glad to be on top of the ridgeline with no casualties. We had destroyed thirty-seven bunkers, two hundred rounds of 82mm mortars, RPGs (rocket-propelled grenades), artillery rounds, and several pounds of rice.

That night, we received orders to go to the flats and get on APCs. First Platoon returned to the CP, and Second Platoon headed for the flats. We hadn't gone two hundred meters when we walked into seventeen more bunkers. We hurriedly destroyed them and moved on. When we arrived at the flats, the APCs were waiting for us, and we returned to Ca Lou for showers, hot chow, and clean clothes.

From there, my platoon was airlifted to Khe Sanh while the rest of the company stayed behind. I wasn't sure where they were or what they were doing, but Second Platoon was alone. I had started with thirty-five men. Six had gone home and there were only two replacements. Anywhere from two to six men stayed in the rear with immersion foot, bee sting, or cellulitis. I was averaging twenty-five to twenty-seven men, although I was authorized forty-five.

For the next ten days, everything went well, except for the heat and insects. Colonel Sutton came out twice in that period and praised us for doing such a good job. The rest of the battalion were finding very little, and their casualty count was high. Bravo Company had found a regular NVA R-and-R camp which was bigger than Second Platoon's find, but they were company-sized. Recon was the only one with a confirmed body count of the enemy, but it also had the most casualties, and we had none in Second Platoon.

The day after the colonel left was resupply. When the resupply birds showed up, there were seven bright-red mailbags aboard. Everyone got about a dozen packages. One thing I didn't worry about was mail call. Each position took a turn pulling guard so they all had ample time to read their mail. I received my Pepsi, Kool-Aid, cigarettes, and two pairs of leather gloves from home. The bags were full of care packages and a two-to-three-week backlog of newspapers. It was a real mess. We had just gotten all spread out when higher called and said they would airlift us out in fifteen minutes.

Now, it was no trouble to hurry and pack because we were used to it by then, but there was no way we could pack all the paper, so we threw it everywhere. We barely made it in time for the birds. We boarded up, not knowing where we were going.

The S-3 (air operations) was flying around and saw our mess, and when we landed at Khe Sanh, he followed us in. I got the worst chewing of my life for the mess we had left on the hill. My father was the only living man who could talk to me that way, so I argued with the major. He was the first football-lineman type I had met, but size made no difference when I was mad.

"Let's go talk to the colonel," he suggested.

"Fine ... anytime," was my answer.

As we were walking away, I heard Floyd say, "I got your mess right here," and I knew he was grabbing his pecker.

The colonel gave me a slight reprimand and excused Major Mailbags. He burst into a big smile, shook my hand, and said, "I have all my best officers in the field, and only the duds are in the rear."

I explained the mess we left and told the colonel that I would do almost anything he asked of me, but the mail for the men was very important. They may have left a few funny papers on a hill in Vietnam, but I wasn't a bit sorry because some of my hometown papers were there, also, and I would have loved to have read them.

He told me that for once I was going to get a break. He had chosen my platoon to guard General Berry for a while, and I was to report to the general's command post as soon as possible. I asked him where the rest of the company was, and he showed me on his big map and said they would be along in a couple of days. He told me that if I had men who looked anything like a Vietnamese, they wouldn't be allowed at the general's compound. So Tang stayed behind. He was due for two weeks' leave anyway. Then we moved into a regular hootch with cots and walls.

I reported to General Berry and was interviewed by him for a solid hour. A finer man I never met. I had no idea of his importance in the war effort, but he was a true gentleman and soldier.

I was to be in charge of all of what we called REMFs, from cooks to engineers, in a complete circle perimeter around the general. A sergeant drove me around the perimeter in the general's jeep and told me I could deploy my men any way I saw fit. All the other men would see me at formation and posting of the guard, but for now I was to get a shower, clean clothes, and a steak. I hadn't thought about a steak for so long that I could smell and taste it right then and there.

The REMFs treated us very respectfully. After eating, we caught a couple of hours' rest and then stood in formation. I placed all the cooks and the rest of the REMFs around the perimeter.

All went well until about midnight when all hell broke loose. I ran from bunker to bunker asking what the hell was going on. Every time I got to one of Second Platoon's bunkers, I found them calm and looking out, but not firing. The sky was being illuminated by candle power, and I could see for a long way. Nothing was moving. Every time I got to an REMF bunker, I found them firing at will. I wished I had one of those wooden paddles the drill sergeants used on everybody's helmets in basic training.

At Fort Campbell in basic training, when we were on the firing line the first few times, the drill sergeants carried long wooden paddles. If a man did anything wrong, he could expect a hard knock on his helmet. I was fortunate not to carry any intelligence knots on my head. They were usually reserved for city boys who had never seen or fired a rifle.

I returned to my own little command post and asked Irons what was going down. He told me that about three miles away at the airstrip some sappers had broken through and were trying to blow up some C-130 airplanes and slicks. They were thought to be in one of our deuce-and-a-halfs driving around and throwing satchel charges at planes.

I told him to put the word out to the platoon to hold fire unless they were sure of what they were shooting at.

"It could be friendly fire in this cluster-fuck," I told Irons. "Also, try to get those damned REMFs to cease fire. But don't take any chances."

I was headed for the main gate, the only place not protected by concertina wire and fougasse. To get there, I had to run by the general's tent. The sky was lit up like yellowish daylight, but I could see well enough to run. As I went around the general's tent, I tripped on a tent stake and fell flat on my face.

The general asked me what was happening, and I explained about the sapper attack on the airstrip. He asked what all the perimeter shooting was about. I assured him that none of Second

Platoon was firing a shot, but those damned REMFs were having a ball wasting ammunition. He asked what a REMF was and I hesitated a second. He told me he was an old soldier and had heard just about everything imaginable, so I told him it was a term that stood for rear-echelon motherfuckers. He broke up laughing and told me to carry on.

I ran over to the main gate where Charlie Kress, Wheeler, and Burford were positioned. I told them not to let any vehicles through without checking with me first and to be on the lookout for a wild deuce-and-a-half.

"What if a general wants to pass?" Charlie Kress asked me.

"Hold him at gunpoint until I get here," I said. General Berry had told me in his briefing that nobody was expected after dark.

"Don't worry, Lieutenant," Charlie assured me. "No one will pass."

I'm glad no one did try to pass that night because I'm sure Burford, Wheeler, and Kress would not have allowed it without a fight.

About 3 A.M., everything quieted down and I got my usual three hours sleep. At 6 A.M., the general called for me, so I put on my shirt and walked over to his tent. There were two captains and a major, none of whom I had seen before. The major was briefing the general, and I got to listen in.

They had killed nine sappers that night and had wounded several more. The sappers had stolen a two-and-a-half-ton truck, but they had only done minor damage with their satchel charges since they were percussion instead of shrapnel type. Thirteen regular NVA had been killed on the southwest perimeter by an Army unit. Seven VC were killed on the northwest perimeter by a platoon. These were probably the diversionary troops for the sappers. Six sappers had been wounded and captured.

At no time had any enemy been close to the general's compound. He said he hoped the NVA didn't start using shrapnel.

Then he said, "Better order more ammunition for the REMFs."

The major looked bewildered.

"Tell him, Lieutenant," the general smiled.

"Sir, your rear-echelon motherfuckers fired up most, if not all, of your ammunition last night shooting at tilleflu birds."

The captain bit and asked what a tilleflu bird was.

"Whatever they were shooting at," I said, "they fired at it till he flew."

The general laughed and said he hated to see my platoon leave. "You should be able to see why I request a grunt platoon each night to be in charge of my perimeter," he said.

I thought about General Berry as I headed for the barracks. I was impressed with the man in the few short hours I'd worked with him. With concerned men like him, it could be nothing but a plus for our side.

When I walked into the barracks, about half the men were asleep on the floor, and the other half were playing Spades.

At noon we rucked up again. Another platoon was unloading at the same time. One of the men in the other platoon mentioned the common expression heard many times a day in Vietnam: "War is hell." And the familiar return from one of ours was, "It sure is, but contact is a real motherfucker." Then the familiar peace and victory signs were exchanged.

For the real grunt fighting in Nam, these were familiar happenings, and the sincerity was ever-prevalent. The REMFs, as a whole, could not understand all that was in those exchanges. Only a grunt knew. Not that the REMFs were never shot at or wounded. But they didn't hump a hundred pounds every day or fight the insects and the jungle, and the lonely feeling of going nowhere with only twenty or thirty men to rely on.

A fire fight for the infantry in the jungle consisted of a few seconds of contact. Generally, the enemy wasn't seen, so firing was kept to a minimum. Within minutes, if not seconds, we had artillery on call, as well as the Air Force gunships. Basically, the whole world was at our fingertips.

Each man only carried about two hundred rounds of ammunition. We seldom fired a weapon for fun because of the fear of running out of ammo. But the REMFs had thousands of rounds. At General Berry's perimeter, they fired more ammo in three hours than an infantry platoon fired on its whole tour of duty. If they had been burdened with a heavy ruck in the jungle, they wouldn't have wasted so much.

The trip back in the deuce-and-a-half took us close enough to the airstrip to see some of the damage. There were two slightly damaged helicopters, and several men were working on the tail end of a C-130. It amazed me what a sapper would go through to damage an airplane. It was as close to a suicide mission as you could get. Although the odds were against him, I understood the action to a certain extent. They were fighting a war, and according to the media, we were only engaged in a conflict.

We found our bunkers and spread out for the evening to relax and write a few lines home. I received word from the colonel to ruck up immediately. A recon patrol from Echo Company was in bad trouble and needed help. Since our platoon was handy, we got the job.

We got to the helipad quickly and checked out our ammunition. Several of the men were either on R-and-R or had immersion foot. This left me twenty-two, which wasn't even half the strength I should have had. We had a new scout to replace Tang, and Tex Lissenbee was working with him. Then we were loading up and heading for the hills again.

7

Our LZ was hot with AK-47 fire from three directions. It was on the side of the hill, so the choppers couldn't quite land. A pilot never completely stopped on a hot LZ, and there were only a few seconds to jump. With good timing a man only had a few feet to fall, but if he was off, it might have meant a fifteen- to twenty-foot jump.

I threw my ruck out and jumped on it, falling about ten feet. Lieutenant Sloan, a man with whom I'd gone through OCS, helped me up. He was sure glad to see me and just kept pumping my hand. I told him to get to the top of the hill and we could talk later. By the time the whole platoon got to the top, we had an hour of daylight left. We made a small perimeter and dug some belly-hiders.

Lieutenant Sloan had followed me in-country about a week later because of leave time. Captain Matts talked him into taking Echo Company, which was recon in an infantry battalion. They usually worked in five- to seven-man teams. This was a seven-man team, and they were short on ammunition and had gotten no sleep in three days. They had been huddled on the hilltop all day waiting for help, and they looked like walking death.

Recon traveled light, so their food supply was gone and so was their water. Without a proper LZ they couldn't get a bird in to pick them up. They had run into several NVA and were being chased along the ridgeline and had stopped to breathe. One of them had noticed the hillside, and Sloan had called for a bird, but enemy fire was too heavy. There was fear that loading seven men would take too long, and they didn't want to take the chance of leaving one or two behind.

We had not been fired upon since the drop, and we could still see, but another quarter-hour meant darkness. Sloan asked if his men could take the night off and get some sleep, and I consented. About that time, without his knowledge or mine, two of his men and Tex Lissenbee, and the scout, left our perimeter.

There was a trail about twenty-five meters away which was heavily used by the NVA. I still don't know exactly why they went over to see that trail, but when they got there they were ambushed. When Sloan and I heard the firing, we went to that side of the small perimeter and asked what happened. No one was sure, but we could hear someone yelling for help.

I called Sergeant Cuevas over and told him that I was taking ten men and going down to help. I'm not sure who the ten were, but I know Sloan and I went, and of course, Doc Wilson, Kenny Irons and Charlie Kress were also there. I couldn't see the rest because it was almost dark.

I led the way. It was slightly downhill so we went faster than I wanted to, but the yelling sounded desperate.

"You'd better speak American or you're dead!" I heard Tex yell as I came to the path.

I spoke clear English. Tex and the scout came over quickly. One recon was dead and the other wounded several times.

We made another small perimeter. I called Cuevas and told him not to fire in our direction for any reason. We were going to spend the night on our bellies as he was to do. There couldn't have been seventy-five feet between us, but in the jungle that was a long way.

Doc informed me that the dead recon was Sergeant Truax and the other man was Sergeant Trunsdale, hit three to five times. Doc thought one round might have gone through a shoulder and come out his back. Two or three shots hit him in the face and one in the throat. He said the verdict wasn't good, but he would try to keep him alive until a medevac could come. Charlie Kress assisted Doc, and I lay down by Sloan and called for a medevac. When I got hold of battalion, they said there was no way they could come because they were socked in by fog.

"Bullshit!" I yelled into the radio. I could count every star in the sky. "If you don't send one quick, a man's gonna die."

They said they'd send one only if they found a volunteer. For the next two hours we waited for an answer. Sloan kept trying to get one. Doc had given the man morphine, which he wasn't supposed to do, but he couldn't control the pain without it. I talked to Trunsdale for a while and he repeated over and over again, "My dad is a major. Please tell him what happened so he can kick ass."

I returned to Sloan, and suddenly a voice came over the radio, loud and clear.

"I'm Snoopy and will relay messages for you." He was in a small aircraft high over us. We could see his strobe light blinking. He assured us they had found two volunteers, and they were on their way, but it would be awhile. They were going to fly a road into Laos until the fog lifted; then they would come back to us above the fog.

"Fine," I told him. "Just get them here because he isn't going to live long if you don't."

For the next hour and a half, we waited. Doc and Charlie were sitting up, taking care of the sergeant. It was a scary feeling to see Charlie Kress outlined in the night holding an IV. One shot would have finished him and another would have taken Doc. I thought that was really brave, and I made a note to write those men up if I made it back myself.

Old Snoopy kept talking to us. Lieutenant Sloan and I were dying to light up a smoke, but we knew the NVA. If they were smart, they would be watching for anything to shoot at.

At about 11:30, we had radio contact with the medevac. I asked for a basket to lace the wounded soldier in.

"No way!" came the reply. "Either throw the man on board or forget it."

He sounded like he meant it. When I hurried over to Doc, I was told the man had just died. I informed the pilot and he took off. I was a little ticked off at first, but after thinking about it, I understood the pilot. He had risked his own life and his crew when he didn't have to, and if I knew who he was today, I would like to shake his hand and tell him thanks for trying.

A chopper had no radar, and to fly along the road for several miles into Laos and then back meant he had to fly low and with his lights on. Undoubtedly, he took a lot of fire both ways. From the men of Second Platoon, Delta Company, Third of the 187th, we salute you and your crew.

Snoopy said goodnight and told us he would be flying around and to call if we needed him. I thanked him but hoped that wouldn't be necessary.

At about 2 A.M., Sloan and I lit up. We shielded each other and then cupped the cigarettes in our hands. Mine was a Marlboro from home, and I thought that if I was going to die, at least I had my Pepsi, Kool-Aid, gloves, and Marlboro cigarettes.

Sloan and I spent the rest of the night wondering what the next day would bring. I knew that twenty-five meters wasn't very far, but under fire it was more like a hundred miles. We made sure everyone was awake just before daylight. Our idea was to return to Sergeant Cuevas and the rest of the platoon at the same time. If we were not fired upon, then we could return for the bodies.

We called Cuevas at daylight and told him we were coming and not to fire for any reason. We made it without a shot. Once we were all located and the danger of shooting each other was over, the men returned for the bodies. Some of the others started cutting an LZ to take recon and the bodies out. We covered the bodies with a couple of ponchos and waited. Those were the first American dead I had seen. It really troubled me to think that any of my men could have been lying there, including myself. It was bad enough that they were Americans, but at least I hadn't known them personally.

At 9 A.M., three NVA walked into our perimeter, apparently unaware of our presence. Charlie Kress, Brent Burford, and Jim Stacy fired them up. I crawled over to see what had happened. They said they had killed one and wounded another, but they didn't know about the third one. Although it was hard to tell in the jungle, I could see the dead body just a few feet away.

Several of the men lined up and fired into the jungle, then we threw a hand grenade. I thought there was no way that anyone could have lived through that.

I started crawling toward the body. Sergeant Broussard was behind me, and maybe someone else. When I got within ten feet, the NVA jumped up and emptied his AK-47, all thirty rounds, and cut down a banana tree between my feet and Broussard's head. I aimed and shot the man eighteen times.

We brought the body back to the LZ and reported the enemy KIA. There wasn't a doubt in my mind that there was at least one more dead out there, but I sure wasn't going to look for him. We stripped the body, as told, and sent in all the information. The man didn't have much on him, but we called in everything right down to the color of his skivvies.

It was then I met Ranger. I had heard about him from the time I had come to the battalion. He was on his third tour of duty and had lived through all kinds of trouble. It was said that he was kill-crazy and could never go back to the States. I can attest to that fact. He started kicking the dead NVA, then he pulled the man's shorts down, took out his knife, and was going to cut off his testicles.

"Don't do it!" I yelled, but he just laughed.

"You cut that body and I'll blow your arm off," I told him. He let go of the genitals and grabbed an ear.

"Sloan, you'd better stop him or I'll shoot," I said.

Sloan talked him out of it, but Ranger pulled his .45 and

shot the dead NVA one more time, and then walked away giving me a crazy stare. Sloan said I was crazy to interfere with Ranger.

"And besides, two of my men are dead," he tried to rationalize.

"It doesn't matter how many are dead," I answered. I couldn't watch mutilation of any kind. Sloan didn't like it, either, but he said Ranger was dangerous and he had to work with him every day. I told him he had better send him to a psycho ward because he was bad luck. Some people lived through anything while people all around them were dying. If he had been in my platoon, I would have gotten rid of him somehow.

We finished cutting the LZ, and the choppers were on the way. The five recons got on the first bird, and we lifted the two dead into the second bird. Then we rucked up and left the area, retracing recons' steps toward a higher place. I had come to like high ground because we controlled the air and could defend it better.

About one hundred meters from the battle scene, we found a hilltop that suited us, and we quit early to dig in. Our orders were to go farther, but high ground and deep holes didn't come along very well after dark, and I felt like regrouping for a while. The men had different looks on their faces; everyone was quiet and very serious. We had lost our scout when the helicopter took the bodies out. At the last second, he had grabbed the bird's skid and crawled in. I knew then that we were in heavy shit, and I had no desire to hunt the enemy until we had time to get over the shock.

While we were digging in, a few dinks were seen in the area we had vacated. A Cobra gunship came in and blew the area away. They reported three killed, and we were supposed to go back and check it out. I told higher we would be glad to. I was asked for a report about an hour later, and I told them the jungle was so thick that we didn't find the bodies.

"If they saw three dead, then they must've seen them from the air," I informed higher. "We saw nothing from the ground."

I figured it would have been pretty stupid to check out the area. I wasn't going to split up the platoon to search for dead NVAs with only twenty-one men. Twenty-one split didn't leave a very big element of firepower. If we had been company-sized, it would have been different. I was always told to let the dead rest, and since they weren't ours, we let them rest. We had credit for one KIA on the records. Helping the career people didn't make sense to me.

I didn't disclose a lot of my thinking to the platoon. If a mission made no sense to me, then I didn't let the men in on it. At that point, none of my men were dead or wounded, so I felt good inside, and that's all that mattered. If something could have been gained for the glory of God and country, I might have felt differently. But my philosophy had been changing.

I had studied several books on guerrilla warfare. It seemed to me that we were fighting a conventional war in a guerrilla jungle. We had everything on our side, by the book, but we were losing men every day.

We were living in the jungle and our mission was to search and destroy. Reconnaissance located the enemy and our superior firepower was to destroy him. The problem seemed to lie in the fact that Americans died when the NVA were found.

Our reconnaissance reminded me of fishing our old pond for yellow-bellied catfish. You had to have a strong pole, very strong fishing line, and a good hook. The ultimate bait for a catfish was a big juicy worm.

If you wanted to be sure to catch some fish, you set out several poles around the pond, and then set up a command post so you could watch all the lines at the same time. If you had a pole in the wrong place, the little schools of fish just nibbled and chewed until you lost your bait. To catch the big cats, you placed two worms on a hook and went to the mud bottoms and waited. Every thirty minutes or so, you checked your bait, and if it was still there, you just moved a few feet and tried again. It wasn't a question of whether you would catch a yellow-belly. It was a matter of when you would catch one and at what expense to your bait box.

After being in the bush for a few long weeks, I had decided that we, the good old American draftees, were the bait. Whether we were nibbled on, chewed, or swallowed whole, depended on where we were dropped in a new place.

There were a lot of big battles fought. More enemy were killed than friendly, but in the jungle it was a different story. Survival was what mattered. Going back to the real world in one piece counted more than anything.

Had I sent men after those dead bodies, I could have lost them. I didn't feel that a few enemy belongings were worth one American finger, let alone a life.

It was hard for me to accept the silly games that were played. For a chopper pilot to get a confirmed body count, a grunt had to risk his life to report them dead. I was sure that by the time it got back to the States, one enemy killed became a dozen.

8

A helicopter came and two men got off to replace Privates Palmer and Smith, who were sick for no apparent reason. Sergeant Hill and Sergeant Gustafson were E-5s fresh from the States. I had twenty-one men in the field, but I suddenly had four sergeants for two squads.

That night was windy and rainy. We couldn't have heard enemy movement no matter what. I called for artillery to fire my NDP and they said it would be awhile because they were firing missions for C Company.

We flipped one radio over to Charlie Company to listen. Someone had gone to sleep and some NVA had crawled inside their perimeter. They were company-sized, with about eighty men. If they had had all the men that a company was authorized, there should have been about two hundred. They were only about one klick away from us.

During that night, they had five KIA and four WIA. I was really nervous because it had happened to eighty men. It made my twenty-one seem like an awfully small element. We kept 50 percent alert at all times. Angel Ruiz got a little jumpy and fired a few rounds. I wasn't too disturbed because the enemy would know we were awake if they were out there.

I lay down for a little sleep and told Irons to wake me when they got ready to fire artillery. He woke me up at 5 A.M. and told me he couldn't stay awake. I asked him why he hadn't wakened me, and he said that he'd tried but I was zonked out. At 5:30 A.M., we woke everyone up and had 100 percent alert. False dawn was about 5:45 A.M. and that was when all hell broke loose. Four RPGs and four hand grenades were lobbed on us. I don't know how much other stuff came at us, but it lasted about twenty seconds and then the enemy ran.

Sergeant Gustafson and Wheeler jumped up and threw hand grenades in the general direction. I cussed aloud about the artillery not firing during the night, but Irons said they had and that he had adjusted it. I'd slept right through everything.

I contacted them and they fired gun one. When the HE or high explosive rounds went off, they were awfully close. Almost too close. I looked at Irons and he grinned.

"Close, isn't it?" he said.

I adjusted it a little closer and then bracketed the area, and they fired about fifty rounds for us. Some were Willie Pete or white phosphorus. It was like the Fourth of July when WP went off. Wheeler jumped up with his camera to take a picture and I came unglued. Two men pulled him back in his foxhole.

After the artillery quit, my orders were to check out the area and to retrace recon's steps. Tex came over to my CP and volunteered to walk point.

"It's not your turn," I told him, but he insisted. He was my best point-man. Davis, Loughan, and Rosencranse were all capable men with experience, but Tex Lissenbee had that little extra. We both agreed that we were in pretty heavy shit. I told him to take his time, even if we traveled only one hundred feet that day. Sergeant Cuevas would walk the middle as usual, and the two new sergeants would bring up the rear.

After about an hour, Tex stopped. I was walking third, so I came up to Tex and saw a used trail following the top of the ridgeline and an open area that would expose us all. I lined the whole platoon up along the open area. We took half the platoon halfway across and hit the dirt. The other half joined us. Then we all ran across the second half as quickly as possible. We set up a small circle and rested.

Tex, Irish Wagner, and I went to the trail and looked it over carefully. We found four grenades and knee prints along the side where they had set an ambush for us. If we had come down that trail, we might have had a few casualties. We had made the right decision, though either one could have killed us. We owed Tex one for that.

While setting up our NDP, we could hear ducks quacking and once in a while a cow bawling. According to my map, there was no village within fifty miles of us, yet there was no way that those animals could have been wild. I reported to higher that we suspected an enemy village or base camp. They told us to recon the area first thing in the morning and report back.

Once again I thought that an element of twenty-one men was pretty small to split up. I requested support from higher and they turned me down. I couldn't fire artillery because the village was right below me. I requested that I move out of the area so artillery could blow it away, and again I was turned down. I knew that I wasn't going to the bottom of the hill with twenty-one men. Whatever was down there was unfriendly and subject to being shot.

I talked it over with Cuevas and Irons, and they agreed not to go in. That night, Irons and I called the artillery from our NDP. We adjusted it almost on top of us, trying to kill the ducks and cows. Back home, a cow bawling at night was music to my ears, but in Vietnam at that time, it could have meant death.

I don't think the arty unit did much good, but at least the NVA didn't sleep either.

All night long I fought with the decision to go or stay. I was sure the enemy knew how many men were camped on the top of the hill. My thoughts brought me to one fact. If the enemy were scared, they would move out, livestock and all, during the night. If they thought they could ambush us, they would be primed and ready. A properly lain ambush could wipe out twenty-one men in about fifteen seconds.

I could still hear the ducks at daylight, and I decided I wasn't going down there without more men. I don't know how much of my quandary the platoon was aware of, but I had made up my mind that whatever was at the bottom of the hill wasn't going to get a piece of my ass.

Just when we thought things couldn't be worse, they took another bad turn. Bravo Company was catching hell, and Colonel Sutton and his pilot took off in the fog and flew into a mountain side, killing them both.

Our new commander, Lieutenant Colonel Steverson, was cavalry, a tank commander in an infantry battalion. I had respected Colonel Sutton highly, and I took an immediate dislike to the new CO. We became friends later, but I didn't like our first dealings. He ordered us into the village and then called me on the radio, telling me to get ready because some birds would pick us up in fifteen minutes. I asked for new coordinates and was refused. I was glad I wasn't going to recon the village, but

I didn't like being airlifted without coordinates. I told him we wouldn't load up without the grid coordinates. He was as mad as a wet bear, but finally he gave me the facts.

Our mission was to find downed helicopters about seven hundred meters from the Laotian border, and the LZ would be a hot one. I told him I only had twenty-one worn-out men and asked if we would have support, but the answer was negative; however, as soon as we got the bodies out, we would return to Khe Sanh for a couple of days rest. We rucked up and waited for the birds.

I was on the first bird as we approached the LZ, which was nothing more than a burned-out bomb crater. We were welcomed by .51 fire, and the bird took two rounds. We could also see green AK-47 tracer coming at us, and the helpless feeling came over me again.

We bailed out and hit the dirt fast. The second bird was also under heavy fire, but all five men got off. The third bird took such heavy fire that it left. Two men jumped from twenty feet, the others stayed in. I didn't know where the rest went, but I was down to twelve men, none of whom were point-men. As I lay there surveying the situation, some Air Force planes flew over and dropped some bombs. They landed one hundred meters behind me and shook the ground. The next birds dropped theirs about one hundred meters in front of us. I yelled to the colonel that our own Air Force had me bracketed and would destroy us all with the next bombs.

He said he'd straighten them out. His little Loach flew right over us and dropped a red smoke for the big boys. They hit their target that time, and I breathed a little easier.

I took the point and headed for the downed helicopter. When we found it, things weren't what I'd expected. The chopper was burned to a crisp and so were the bodies. They were grotesque. One had his arms up in the air and had burned in that position. Sergeant Broussard put an extra pair of socks on his hands, and I had my leather gloves. We placed the bodies in our ponchos. The sight and feel of those men will live with me forever.

We were receiving small-arms fire and mortars the whole time. The Air Force was bombing. I was sick and was pretty sure Broussard was, too. The other ten men opened fire on three dinks, but we didn't have time to see if we got any. I began to feel as if we were the only grunt platoon left in Vietnam, and it was more like a recon element than it was a platoon.

We returned to the LZ and a bird came in for the bodies. We literally threw them on board. He was taking heavy fire the whole time. I thanked God for the noise of the chopper because it made it difficult to hear the bullets.

We took heavy AK fire for about ten minutes, then I received word to go to the top of the hill for the night. My asshole was already so tight I couldn't stand it, but we had no choice but to tighten up even more.

I headed for the top of that hill with eleven of the tiredest men I'd ever seen. I knew then how Sloan had felt when we'd rescued him. As I approached the crest, I walked into a GI from Third Platoon. He knew I was coming up the hill, but no one had told me they were there. I had my weapon on full rock 'n' roll, and why I didn't shoot him I'll never know for sure. Perhaps my childhood saved that man's life. Dad had always told me never to fire a gun into the brush unless I recognized the game 100 percent. The first thing I saw was the GI steel pot, and my mind must have clicked positively.

"You better speak American or you're dead," I called to him.

"Don't shoot!" he yelled.

My M-16 was aimed at his forehead, but I took my finger slowly from the trigger.

We entered the perimeter and found Captain Edwards, Lieutenant Powers, Lieutenant Johnson, and Mike Dalton. We dropped our heavy rucks and collapsed.

"Where are the rest of your men?" Edwards asked.

"I don't have any idea, but I think they're safe," I answered. The rest of the company had two downed helicopters. One group was dead, the others were alive.

"How long have you been on the hill?" I asked.

"Two to three hours," came the answer.

They had been listening to our fire fights the whole time. I was too tired to be upset. I asked that my men be allowed to rest for the night.

"No problem. Just be ready if you're needed," Edwards said.

It seemed like ages since I'd seen Mike, but actually it had only been a few days. We had both aged tremendously. I asked Mike what it was all about.

"I don't know," he answered. "But I'm tired of going from one place to the next and not accomplishing anything, anywhere."

"If I die, would you please remember forever that I died trying?" I asked him.

"The same goes for you too, Don," was his answer.

Only those who were there could have understood our inner feelings. We'd been in-country only thirty days, and at the rate we were going, none of us would survive. I counted all the luck we'd had up until then.

"There's no way we can make it for a solid year," I said. "If we don't get killed or wounded, the physical and mental strain will get us."

Mike missed his wife and future kid in the worst way, and I missed mine, but time didn't permit loneliness to linger in the jungle. I opened a can of fruit cocktail and asked Mike what he'd been through. His story was similar to mine except he hadn't got a steak or met General Berry. He was unhappy with the captain because he was lost all the time.

"Do you know where we're at now?" I asked.

"About seven hundred meters from Laos."

"Seven hundred meters would be in a lot lower country than we are in now," I said as I got out my map.

We traced a few azimuths and studied the map. We decided that if we weren't in Laos, we were so close that we could have tossed a silver dollar across the border.

We called Powers over and he agreed. When we approached Captain Edwards, he disagreed, and said the colonel himself had given him the coordinates.

"Just maybe we were lied to," I said. "Ask the artillery to fire a smoke round."

He finally agreed, but the colonel interrupted and told us we didn't need artillery fired for location. The CO believed us then because there was no reason not to fire for us.

The choppers came for us the next morning. The rescued pilots were on the first bird and I was on the second. The third bird, with Cuevas on board, was shot down, and we circled back to watch. Everyone got off safely, however, and another bird came in to pick them up. The rest went off without a hitch. When we reached Khe Sanh, I was met again by Major Mailbags. He chewed me out for calling him a dumb ass. I didn't remember doing it, but in the heat of battle he was lucky that was all I called him.

My mother-in-law always told her grandchildren that if they spat on their bait, it would bring them good luck. I vowed that day that neither Major Mailbags nor anyone else would ever spit on me again.

A coldness set into me. My men were not worms to be spat on. We were the ultimate bait, and we deserved all the respect in the world. Colonel Steverson gained my respect that day, but Mailbags could never earn it.

Our only danger at Khe Sanh was the rounds which the NVA were firing directly over us at the airstrip. Several rounds fell short and some were duds. The few REMFs we had with us would scuttle around like rats when the old familiar "whoosh, whoosh" went over. The grunts would laugh and say, "Look at those REMFs run!" We all knew where every bunker was and could have run just as fast if we'd needed to.

We spent some days doing nothing but drinking beer and dodging short rounds. It angered me because each day the men were getting more and more itchy to get back to the jungle. They were getting tired of the first sergeant and lifers like Mailbags playing army in a war zone.

"Tell your men to shave. Keep your bunkers clean. Can't your men act a little more military?"

Every night, we were briefed on what was happening to the rest of the battalion. Things were fairly quiet for a while.

On the eighth night, the colonel and captain got me in a jeep and took me over to the tank command. It was a jeep ride I'll never forget.

Khe Sanh was a plateau in the middle of the mountains. We drove down a road which wound around the side of the plateau, and I saw a mechanized division dug into the side of Khe Sanh. Although I was no judge of the size of a mechanized unit, I thought it had to have been at least a division.

Caterpillars had been working day and night, digging holes for tanks and other equipment. I knew that if every dink had seen this up close, they would have thrown up their hands and *"Chou hoi'd"* immediately. The equipment wasn't worth much in the jungle, but it could run the roads and protect Khe Sanh.

We pulled up in front of a large building with guards everywhere. I hadn't seen that much brass in one place in my life. A full-bull colonel gave the briefing once we'd settled inside. They had located the hill that the NVA were using, and they were going to play hell on the east side of it while an infantry platoon sneaked up the west side armed with grenades and rocket launchers.

The reason I was there suddenly hit me. I wasn't the only lieutenant in the building, but I was the only one with cross-rifles on my collar. We were to leave on APCs (armored personnel carriers) the next morning.

We returned to the Rakkasan's helipad and went into the colonel's briefing room. He asked me what I thought of the mission.

"Two things, colonel. I don't know if a heavily armed platoon can get to the top in one day and do the damage and return. Secondly, there could be several thousand dinks on the hill. My twenty-one-man platoon can only handle ten to one odds, not one hundred to one."

My inner feeling was one of suicide for the platoon, but at least we would be taking something that amounted to a damn. "You'll do it then?" he asked.

"If it's an order, we'll sure try," I responded.

I told the platoon to get two days' supply of rations and to be up at 0500, I informed them we would be carrying extra firepower. Mike and I talked it over and agreed it would be great if it worked, but if it didn't, it would probably be suicide for Second Platoon.

I had written home and asked for a small calendar to carry because the days seemed to run together. When I showed it to Mike, he said it would work, but that it wasn't very funny. It was a three-by-three inch advertising calendar put out by Greenwell Funeral Home, the place that will probably bury me someday, hopefully a long way down the road. Receiving it just before a suicide mission wasn't very comforting

In my left breast pocket was a Bible with a lead plate in it, given to me by my in-laws, and I carried it everywhere. So I put my calendar in my right pocket. I had the Lord in one pocket and my funeral director in the other. Had I been a fatalist, I would have walked sideways from then on, left side first. I was only hoping that Digger Greenwell didn't get me for years to come. In fact, about the time I was boarding the APC, my Dad was probably having evening coffee with Digger.

After about an hour of riding in the APC, the old vulnerability hit me. One properly placed mine or RPG would have killed us all. I always felt better on the ground because I could hide and maneuver so much better.

After we unloaded, we lined up and started up the hill. Tex's father had passed away and he was headed home, so I had twenty men plus a new scout named Vo Van Vo. He was a dandy! He was the most aggressive of all the scouts I'd met. I think fighting had been born into him. He would tell us how many Americans he had killed when he was a VC, and now he wanted to kill NVAs. He was about 90 percent bullshit, but at least he would walk point every day. Every other word was a cuss word. He said we were fucking crazy GIs to be going up that hill.

"Maybe," I said. "But get started anyhow."

About two hours later we got a call to *"di di moi"* back down to the APCs and get our asses out of there. We were only too happy to oblige, and literally ran down the hill. I never did find out why the mission was aborted, but I was glad the monkey was off my back. Rumor had it that the dinks had radioed our division in plain English, saying that my platoon was soon to be buzzard bait. Whatever the reason, I was glad to be back to company-size again. They flew us west, close to Laos again, only this time the ARVNs were coming back and the operation was almost over.

9

According to my schedule, about fifty days had gone by. The men were coming and going in two's and three's. Although I had twenty-seven men assigned to me, I counted only twenty in the field. Immersion foot, VD, fever, and bee stings were still among the reasons.

We set up on an old Marine encampment. It had been built and protected in 1968. They had dug deep foxholes and had lined the walls with dirt-filled ammo boxes. Prior to our landing, the area had been cleared of booby traps by using fire-bombs. All we had to do was clean up the area and make it livable.

While helping dig out Second Platoon's command post bunker, I noticed a small green snake which kept sticking its head out of an old mortar box. I joked about it for a while and finally tired of the game, so I took out my K-bar knife and, while Irons teased it, I cut its head off.

We didn't think much about it, and the snake was too small to eat, so we tossed it into the next bunker.

Several yells greeted us. I'm not sure of all that was said, but I know my grandmother's ears would have burned.

"Nobody should be afraid of a dead, headless, twelve-inch, green snake," I yelled.

A few adjectives later I caught the words "bamboo viper." Kenny and I immediately had a different respect for the snake. I wasn't sure whether the snake was poisonous or if all the rumors were true, but we didn't want to find out

Our rumor was if we were bitten by a bamboo viper, you had three steps before you died. It was nicknamed the three-step snake. I put the word out to be careful. His or her mate might have been around.

A tank sat across the road from our bunkers. Every half an hour during the night, the gunner would fire several rounds of ammo, and several times we saw enemy bullets ricochet off the tank. We were left alone the first two nights, but on the third day we were hit with mortar rounds. Our bunkers were deep and had covers on the tops, and no direct hits were scored. Captain Edwards had a chunk of shrapnel miss his head by inches. We all tasted shrapnel, but he carried his around telling everyone over and over how close it had come. He even wanted a Purple Heart, but none of us would write him up for it.

After about seven days of area reconnaissance with only slight enemy activity, we were getting pretty well relaxed, which was very dangerous. If a person relaxed too much, he could count on the NVA to tighten his bunghole another notch. Even though we didn't see the dinks, we all had enough experience to know that they were watching us and waiting for a mistake.

The mistake came in a way I'd never have expected. We had set up a mechanical on a trail outside our perimeter, and at three in the afternoon we heard it go off. I was sitting in my bunker and writing a letter home at the time. Someone yelled for a medic, and Doc Wilson ran to check it out. I thought the colonel would get a body count because few animals roamed around during the day, except two-legged ones.

One of the troopers came running over to me, saying that Wheeler had walked into the ambush.

"That's impossible," I told him. "That was my mechanical, and he helped me string the wire and set it up."

Wagner told me that he had one leg and an arm severed, and one eye was completely out of the socket. I was stunned and didn't know what to say or do. I started towards the ambush, but Wagner and Irons stopped me. They said that Doc was taking care of it and there was nothing I could do.

Irons gave me the radio and I asked Doc what the verdict was. He told me there was no way he was going to live, and he asked for permission to ease the pain with morphine.

"Do what you can, Doc," I answered. "The choppers are on their way."

Wheeler was the same as gone when the medevac got there, but he was sent in, barely alive. Even though I had nothing to do with the incident, I felt responsible, and it left me hollow inside.

Doc told me he wasn't sure what had happened, but he suspected drugs. It was the only way he could explain why a man would knowingly walk into a mechanical, apart from suicide, and Wheeler hadn't seemed like the type.

I never questioned the platoon about the incident. I was sure that some of them had to know something, but if they did, they kept quiet. I had lost my first man, and it hadn't been to the enemy.

I told the CO that Wheeler had apparently gone to take a crap and went farther than he should have. I didn't tell him that he'd had no weapon or steel pot with him.

I found a secluded spot and sat down with my thoughts. I had heard all the rumors about drugs in Vietnam, but I had never taken any, including marijuana, so I didn't know the effects. I had been in the bush forever, and I couldn't imagine using drugs when everyone's lives depended on alertness and quick reaction. I hadn't been close to Wheeler like I was with some of the men, and for that I will always carry the guilt that he might not have done what he did had I known him better.

My platoon had been to see the Elephant, with no casualties, while every other outfit had taken its share. I felt that my men had been good and had tried to do their job well. But now some of my pride was waning. I had to find out if there was more trouble in my platoon that I thought.

When we were on two-day stand-downs, some of the men smoked a little, and some got a little drunk, myself included. But it was a different story in the bush. I had one man who smoked grass all the time. When we went to the jungle, he carried plenty for himself, and everyone knew it. His supply would run out after a couple of days, so he would sprain his ankle and I'd medevac him out. Everyone would laugh at him. I was naïve about drugs and thought he was the only one who smoked and that it was no problem because he spent most of his time in the rear. But I was beginning to wonder about the others.

I needed to talk to Mike. He and I would be able to sit down and rationalize the situation and come up with some type of solution. I decided that I would find out how big the problem was, and though I doubted I could correct it, at least I would know whether to tighten the old asshole another notch. I felt like I was a hundred years old, and I was not happy with life.

The weight on my shoulders was a tremendous load. Someone had to be the scapegoat in a war full of bad publicity, and the career soldier was not likely to take the blame for a mistake. The privates had been drafted and were doing the best they could in a bad situation, so the lieutenants like myself caught a lot of flak from both sides. I would gladly have handed over my commission to anyone who wanted it; in fact, I was getting damned tired of taking orders from someone ten miles away in a bunker. My thoughts had been patriotic when I'd first come in-country, but that patriotism was being tested to the fullest.

My thoughts were broken up by Sergeant Broussard. He informed me that the ARVNs were leaving Laos and all American troops were being crow-hopped back to Khe Sanh. By dark our outfit would be the farthest west before the airlift at daylight.

Sergeant Broussard was the only black in the platoon at the time. At about six o'clock that evening, he jumped up on top of his bunker and said: "Everybody listen. My name is Adam Broussard, and I'm the only black man left in the platoon. I'm the farthest west of any black man in the U.S. Army. If the dinks want my hide, they will have to come to Rainesville, Louisiana. In two weeks, I'm going home, and there ain't nothin' alive that can kill me now."

I went over and talked to Adam for a while. Since he was going home, he could talk freely and I wouldn't repeat anything he told me. He told me that as far as he knew there were only three or four guys who smoked in the field, and that was very seldom. Absolutely no hard stuff. In the rear, at times several smoked a little grass. He also assured me that several of the men would not touch it at any time.

"What happened to Wheeler?" I tried.

"Who knows?" came the answer.

I didn't want to do any injustice to Wheeler, so the best I could say was that he made a mistake and paid for it with his life.

The next day they pulled out the mortar platoon and CO. We stayed one more night, and it was a very long night. The

NVA stepped up their activities as soon as the ARVNs left Laos. Two more tanks came in, so it was Second Platoon and three tanks against the whole NVA, if that was what they wanted. We took incoming rounds the whole night long. One tank was destroyed and another was hit. The next morning we walked down to the road and waited for the slicks beside the remaining tanks.

By 0800, the last of the ARVNs had passed and the tanks followed. Second Platoon was alone again. The birds picked us up at 0900 and took us back to Khe Sanh for a short meal and three hours of rest. It took a week of crow-hopping before the mission was over. We had to endure one last hardship on the sixty-seventh night before we headed for Camp Evans, our home.

There was a small village outside Evans that was sympathetic to the NVA, and it was suspected that several VCs were living there. Our entire battalion surrounded the village at dark. We lay on the ground in a large circle and were told to shoot anyone leaving the village.

One hundred percent alert was in effect. Nobody slept. Illumination was fired all night long so we could see. Not one person left the village, and the next day when the ARVNs went into the town, all they found were six "draft dodgers." Some were only fifteen years old.

The only casualties were a dead baby and a burnt mother. One of the illumination rounds had been short, so it was still burning when it went through the grass roof and fell on mother and child.

We lost a night's sleep and several brownie points because of the village. Several of those people worked at Camp Evans during the day. No wonder they had a tough time deciding who the good guys were.

At 10 P.M., we took a short chopper ride back to Rakkasan headquarters. They were all prepared for us. Tent city had been constructed. We crawled off the birds and the colonel and staff officers were there to greet us. We all lined up and placed our ammo in the proper boxes. Some of it was green with corrosion. There were hand grenades, Claymores, LAWs (light anti-tank weapons), M-79 shells, over-and-under shells, M-16 shells, and .45 shells. We stacked our machetes and rifles, laid our rucks down, and started through tent city.

Lieutenant Griswald looked us over and told us to get a bath and clean clothes. We showered in luxury. Soap was everywhere. In sixty-seven days we had had three showers. The rest were helmet baths. The spirit of Second Platoon was high. The old goosing and swearing was back.

After we showered, we all got haircuts and shaves by real barbers, military barbers! Our clean clothes were not new, but they felt so much better than the rags we took off. In some cases they weren't fit to be called rags. Several of us returned to the medic's tent where we had salve and bandages put on the cellulitis. Some had bandages covering both arms. Brent Burford from Pennsylvania looked like a mummy.

From there, we went to the pay tent and received our two months' pay. I got two hundred dollars. The rest had been sent home. We then returned for our weapons, and as we passed the piles of clothes, we found it hard to believe that we'd been wearing them a short time before. By then, the two Vietnamese girls who sorted clothes were going through the pockets, sorting the good from the bad, and I assure you the bad pile was the biggest by far.

I picked up my M-16 and saw that the barrel was rusted beyond a coat of oil. We had kept the bolts and working mechanisms shined, but the rest had hardly been touched. And I had no insignia on my label to distinguish me from a Pfc. I didn't give it much though, but as I was walking to the barracks, I met Colonel Steverson and Major Mailbags, and the major jumped me about not wearing a rank. I told him we'd just got new clothes and no one had issued any rank.

"Besides, in the bush, I don't need any insignia," I added.

He told me to go to the S-4 and come back looking like a lieutenant. The colonel said there would be a briefing at 1800 hours. Several of the platoon were walking with me at the time.

"Lieutenant," Floyd Kotewa addressed me. "If you want me to, I will get that major tonight."

"No, Floyd," I answered "There is an old Special Forces saying that says we never get even, but we do get closer. It will all work out, and if it doesn't, they can send me home."

I put my M-16 by my bunk and headed for S-4. I met Doc Melson, and right behind him was Major Mailbags.

"How you doin', Red Pecker?" Doc asked.

"Fine," I said. No salutes were exchanged, and the major was really hot under the collar. He chewed my ass royally. I told him that Red Pecker was my call sign in the bush and that I'd told the men not to salute me.

It had been so long since we'd been in the rear that it would take the men some time to become military again. I had told the men to call me Don, lieutenant, or Red Pecker, which had been my nickname since freshman P.E. at good old Casey High School. But somehow I didn't figure the major would understand, so I took my ass-chewing in silence and then went to S-4 to get the proper insignia.

When I returned to the company area at 1600 hours, the beer was flowing. There were horse tanks full of it. It was the first cold beer we had seen in a long while, and it tasted so good. It was almost as good as a cold Pepsi.

Doc Melson asked me what I thought of Major Mailbags and if I wanted him silenced for good.

"Doc, as long as he's in his bunker and I'm in the bush, we won't have a problem," I said. "And if we do, my M-16 can shoot as straight as yours. I told you men that I didn't care what you called me as long as we did what had to be done, and I haven't changed my mind. But while we're in the rear area, you might use 'lieutenant' to save me from ass-chewings. And if a superior officer is around, it wouldn't hurt to salute."

He said he'd pass the word on.

I returned to the lieutenants' barracks and dug out some leech straps. I felt a little naked without them, so I tied them on, even though there were no leeches in the rear. The urge to carry my M-16 was strong, but I couldn't. I left and headed for the chow hall.

On the way, I stepped on a little vial made of clear plastic. I had never seen anything like it before, so I picked it up and was looking at it when Mike came up. He said it was a heroin vial, 90 percent pure stuff. A lot of the rear people were badly hooked. We counted thirty-four more vials on the way to the mess hall. Mike told me I was in for a shock if I didn't believe what I was seeing.

We got our food and sat down at a table for the first time in a while, and it felt funny to pick up a regular fork. Iced tea was served, all we could drink. I drank so much I felt sick, but it sure tasted good.

From there, Mike and I went to the briefing room. I was introduced to Lieutenant Mullens and Lieutenant Caparo, who had been in OCS with Mike. I had been in Ninety-fifth OCS and they'd been in Ninety-sixth, about two weeks behind me. Even though we had never met at Fort Benning, we had been through what we'd thought was hell together. We stood around and talked about OCS and the good times we remembered.

The briefing started when the colonel showed up. In Lam Lon 719 we had twenty-two men killed and 117 wounded. My mind clicked fast: one out of seventeen killed, and one out of three wounded. We were told how many enemy were killed and wounded and were given a long list of captured and destroyed material. It was estimated that we had killed or wounded many more of enemy, but it was not confirmed.

The South Vietnamese gave its highest decoration to our battalion, and there were many more citations coming. All things considered, it looked like we had done a bang-up job. The other battalions had more dead and wounded and had destroyed less than we had, so we were to be commended. There was to be a memorial in two days for our dead and wounded. That night there would be an officers' party to celebrate our victory. Heal up and rest were in order for the next three days.

As soon as the briefing was over, I reported to the colonel. Major Mailbags was there, along with our XO (executive officer), Major White. I hadn't met Major White before, but the grapevine told me he was a square shooter. Colonel Steverson complimented my platoon's action in the operation. He asked me if I could bury the hatchet with Major Mailbags.

"I don't have a problem with the major," I told him. "He seems to have a problem with me. Give my men and me a mission, and we will do it. We've done so in the past. But out in the bush, it's a different story. Help from the rear is appreciated, but if I can't run my platoon firsthand, then they don't need me out there. I'm a red-haired farm boy, and I'm easily angered by some people."

Colonel Sutton had long since forgiven me, and I thought the Mailbags incident was over. He hadn't blamed me for anything I'd done, and in turn, I had held no grudge against anyone. But Major Mailbags persisted at getting on my case. Colonel Steverson got all bent out of shape and jumped the major.

Major White asked me to step outside with him while the colonel finished with Mailbags. White was a fine soldier, so I told him all that had happened.

"Don't worry about it," he told me.

"I don't have anything to worry about, Major. My men are good soldiers, but they will not put up with a lifer who runs in this heat every morning like we were at Fort Benning, Georgia."

"The colonel is working on that right now," he told me. "All will be well in a few days."

10

Although I'd only spent twelve hours at the Rakkasan rear area, it was like home to me. It felt good to have a secure place that I could walk around in.

Rakkasan was set up like the typical battalion, complete with mess hall, VIP barracks, company areas, headquarters, S-1 (personnel), S-2 (intelligence), S-3 (operations), S-4 (supply), and S-5 (civil affairs).

Delta Company was on the west end of the compound. The showers and shitters were around the outer edges of the barracks. The showers were inside a small tin shed with a large overhead tank. The water was lukewarm on hot days and cool on rainy days. The crappers ranged from four-holers to six-holers. They had back doors that raised up where fifty-gallon drums cut in half were slid under the holes.

The papa-san who worked for the battalion spent his entire day mixing diesel fuel with the crap and then burning it. His weekly pay was $3.75 American. He made a dollar more than the women who sorted clothes only because he was a male. Apparently it was all right for women to do men's work, but they had to be paid less. The three workers and our scouts were the only Vietnamese allowed within our perimeter. The workers returned home every evening. They were inspected at the MP station for contraband, both coming in and going out.

I was watching papa-san burn shit in order to learn the art when some of the platoon came up with several cases of beer. We sat down in an open area about twenty yards away from the backside of one crapper. After a few beers and several jokes, someone asked, "Did you see how that one guy wiped his ass?"

Now I'm not saying that we were bored with nothing else

to do, but for the next two hours we drank beer and counted the different styles of ass wiping. We counted seventeen different methods, all of which seemed appropriate for getting the job done.

According to Army issue, we were allowed five squares of toilet paper per day. We should have taken names because some methods required a lot of toilet paper. For example, the "left-hand, then right-hand, then bending-over-while-the-right-hand-goes-between-the-legs" wipe required three different uses of toilet paper. If that man took a daily crap, he would use a seven-year supply of toilet paper in one year's time.

There were also different methods according to rank. The higher the rank, the neater the fold, and the more wasteful the user. We didn't get a chance to view the colonels and majors because they had their own private two-holers. After some quick calculations, we decided that the career soldiers across Vietnam owed the taxpayers $1 million or the equivalent in toilet paper. I don't recommend this activity on a Sunday picnic, but it passed a few hours and we had a few good laughs.

By suppertime, we were all pretty well feeling our oats, so we began to sing. We had a REMF with us who played any instrument he could get his hands on. That day, his guitar only had four strings on it, and one side of his banjo had a hole in it. Private John Sherman from New York had his Jew's harp, and someone had stolen two spoons from the mess hall.

Doc Wilson had his tape recorder, so I bought a tape and started taping the songs. I didn't know about the other guys, but I knew I had no musical ability at all. I was full of music because none had ever come out, but after a few cases of beer I really didn't care.

We had a great time, one that was hard to describe. We watched shit burn, learned several ways to wipe our asses and were shit-faced by midnight. I took my tape and headed for my bunk and luckily woke up in the right one the next morning.

Now, one good thing about a full hangover is you know

for sure that you have to get better, so you look forward to the day and hope for it to be cloudy until noon. I listened to the tape at about noon, and it definitely wasn't a number-one hit on the first half hour. But the drunker we'd gotten, the better it had sounded, and I had to admit that in the last couple of songs, I didn't do too badly on the spoons.

I wrapped up the tape and sent it to my brother, Roy, who was at Southern Illinois University at the time. I dropped a few lines home, took a shower, tried one of my new wiping techniques, and got ready for the 719 celebration at the officers' club.

The officers' club was a small barrack that could barely be called a club. There was nothing to prove that it was a club, except for a small sign over the door and a few bottles of whiskey. The choices were limited for a connoisseur of the alcoholic world. There was a large set of airborne wings that looked like a cup into which Captain Matts poured several different kinds of whiskey and rum and then added orange juice.

After about three hours of hard partying, someone suggested a toast. The colonel had everyone line up according to rank, then he lifted the wings, made a toast, and drank heavily. Each officer drank in turn until it got back to the CO. This went on and on until Lieutenant Mullens, Captain Matts, the colonel, and I were the only ones who hadn't gotten sick or left to fall asleep somewhere.

Finally, the colonel decided he'd had enough—and I hesitate to say our leader staggered—but he used a few extra steps getting out of the building. If there was a winner, I guess Captain Matts would get the honor, but Lieutenant Mullens and I would have given him a run.

I left for bed with an enormous burning rock in my stomach. I knew that sleep was going to be difficult unless I drained off a little, so I sneaked around a corner and upchucked for a while.

Breakfast sat just a little heavy, but other than that, I felt a lot better than I expected after two days and nights of replacing all the fluids I'd lost on Lam Son 719.

That day, we held a memorial service for our dead and wounded. Twenty-two stakes were driven into the ground, and a helmet was placed on each one. The ceremony was brief, but I can still see those helmets in their neat, military row.

My thoughts during the ceremony took me back to Southern Illinois University, 1965. I lived about a block and a half from Old Main, and each day as I walked to classes, there would be a demonstration of some type: "Ban the war in Vietnam, ban the bomb, no nukes, peace for the world. ..." All this activity almost overshadowed the NAACP (National Association for the Advancement of Colored People) fight for equal rights.

I really didn't care to get involved in any of it because we had no blacks in Casey, Illinois, and we hadn't been affected by the Vietnam conflict.

On one particular day, I was headed for the Agriculture Building to take a test on soil. I knew I was going to flunk that test, so I wasn't in a good mood when I passed a group trying to get names on a petition to stop the war in Vietnam.

I was a sophomore at the time. As I tried to pass the group, I was stopped by a young man from Casey who was a freshman. His name was David Wright. He was wearing sandals, blue jeans, a corduroy coat, and a black tie. He had on love beads and peace symbols, and his hair was down to his shoulders.

I knew him from grade school. When I was in sixth grade, he and I, and another student, Brent Owens, slid down the stair banister and got a whipping for it. At least, Brent and I did. David's dad was the school principal, so he just got a reprimand. I didn't like David from then on. Besides, he was what we called "fairy" back then because he liked dancing, cheerleading, and drum majorettes.

So he recognized me that day, grabbed my arm, and pulled me into a circle of what I called peaceniks. I thought every one of them was dressed kind of funny. David introduced me to his friends.

"Here, Don, sign this petition," he said.

"Leave me alone," I said. "I'm not into anything but agriculture and white socks with my suit."

A couple of them started in on how our country was wrong and the youths had to open their eyes before a whole generation of young American men were wiped out. By then, two other "normal" people had been dragged into the circle.

Their first mistake was grabbing me by the arm, and their second mistake was threatening me if I didn't sign. My first mistake was asking them what they'd do if I didn't sign. Their answer caused me to get mad.

"If you don't sign, we'll hold your hand and mark an X," somebody said.

"If you people believe in peace, then you're wrong to force anyone to sign anything," I said. "Fifty people couldn't make me sign."

I pleaded one last time to be left alone. Someone shoved me from behind and I exploded. I hit someone in the nose and a major fight broke out. I was scared, so I was fighting to win.

A few minutes later, the university police took us over to its main building. There were about thirty of us. Only three of us were normal people, according to dress code, so I asked to be separated from the group. The other two followed me to a corner of our own.

"I'll be glad to accept any punishment," I told the police, "as long as I'm not considered a part of those idiots."

We were taken, one at a time, to see a captain. I told my story and was turned loose. None of us received any punishment. And more than five years later, I was in Vietnam, thinking back to those days while we held the memorial service.

We spent the afternoon getting ready for the field. I'd learned a few things on 719, and I told the platoon that anyone who wanted to learn how to call artillery should get a map and

compass, so we could check each other out every day. I went to
the S-4 and asked for extra maps and compasses, but I was told
that only three sets were issued to a platoon and that I already
had all I was going to get. I told the men we would have to
share.

Camp Evans was located in the province of Quang Tri
which was flat as far as the eye could see. The colonel said we
would be heading to the mountains about ten miles off to the
west. We thought we would see little action after 719 because
it would take awhile for the NVA to regroup and resupply. Our
job was to recon, try to cut supply lines, and set up ambushes at
night.

We landed about three ridgelines away from the flats. The
LZ was cold, which was true happiness. I set up our NDP that
evening, and as I was spreading out my map to double check, I
looked up and saw eight men unfolding their maps while compasses dangled from their necks.

"How in the world did you get those?" I asked in astonish-
ment.

"Lieutenant," Kotewa answered, "there are some questions
you don't ask, and there are some things you don't see. We
were authorized three compasses and that's all we have. We
bred the compasses last night and they had babies."

"All right," I said. "Show me where we landed and where
we're at now, and the one who's on target gets to call artillery
tonight."

Some people have a gift for keeping their directions straight
and some have to learn the hard way. Four of the men were
going the wrong direction all day. Two were three klicks off
and one was a klick away from where I put us. Kenny Irons
was within one hundred meters of the coordinates I had shack-
led.

We had a few minutes of daylight left so we shot a few
azimuths and charted our next day's mission. Then we located
the captain and the rest of the friendlies on the map. The men

picked it up quickly, and I knew I had better be pretty sharp from then on because Kenny Irons and a few others were going to be double checking me every step. In fact, after Irons fired the artillery, he might have been closer than I was, but I wasn't going to admit it. Anytime a person is traveling up and down ridgelines, a one hundred-meter error is pretty good map reading.

We reconned the area for the next three weeks and saw very little activity and found very few enemy signs. During that time, the platoon got to be really close. We were averaging seventeen to nineteen men in the field. Some had gone home and there were no replacements.

Doc Wilson received a letter from his girlfriend that upset him to no end. I read the letter and thought it was a really nice one and that there was nothing to be upset about. She had bought a car to get to work in, and he read between the lines and thought she was running the streets. He said he had to get home and marry that girl.

"Doc, you are the best," I told him. "And I don't want to lose you. It's only five-and-a-half months until your tour is up."

"I just can't wait that long," he answered.

I didn't know it, but that was the last day he took a malaria pill.

When it was nearly dark, we got a fox report of one. That was a butthole tightener. Fox reports ranged from one to ten. A ten meant that someone suspected the enemy might be in our area, and then again they might not be, so a fox ten was a joke. But a fox one meant that the enemy had not only been seen but also counted and the weaponry described.

Irons unshackled the report: Nineteen men in black pajamas carrying AK-47s, two machine guns, three radios, at ground coordinates such and such. Those were my coordinates as well, but one hundred meters was a long way in the jungle.

I double-checked the report, thinking some pilot had spotted us, but I thought they'd surely know the difference between black pajamas and U.S. OD (olive drab) green fatigues. We dug a little deeper and waited for daylight.

At about midnight, a mechanical went off. I reported it and was told to check it out.

"Not until daylight," I said.

An unfamiliar voice came over the radio. It didn't sound like old Mailbags. "Is there a reason why you can't or won't check it out?" came the voice.

"Yeah. Nineteen of them. Plus we have other mechanicals set up, and I don't feel like stumbling into them," I explained.

I got a surprise when the voice continued. "This is your new S-3. Check it out at daylight."

"10-4 on that. See you in three days for a beer."

"Who's buying?" he asked.

"Nineteen happy soldiers," I answered. "Welcome aboard!"

Then he offered a dog team to check it out at daylight, and I accepted without hesitation. It was my first chance to work with a dog. A soldier and his shepherd unloaded and came up to me. He said that nobody was to touch the dog unless permission was given.

He explained that his dog was a personnel dog. It could only smell the enemy. No booby traps, just humans.

We checked out the mechanical, and according to the dog, it wasn't a human who had set it off, and sure enough, we had another mongoose. We moved about four hundred meters that day, and it was good to have the dog with us. I realized that dogs could make mistakes, so we kept our guards up, but it was still a very comforting feeling. I had been raised with dogs all my life and had hunted behind some of the best bird dogs and coonhounds in the country, so I had a great deal of faith in a personnel dog. His handler placed his life on the line every day because they walked point and followed blood trails.

We came to a large creek deep enough to swim in, so we broke Army regulations and swam like ten-year-old boys. I started to set up security, but the handler assured me that his dog could detect anyone within a quarter-mile. Much to his disappointment, I still set up some security, though it was a token amount, not nearly as much as normal.

I hadn't been skinny dipping in years. We used to go frogging in the nude out on the farm. We had to go naked so our mothers wouldn't know. Wet underwear would give us away.

Most of us didn't wear the OD green underwear in Vietnam anyway. And we weren't really worried about our mothers finding out. Everyone's arms and faces were brown from the jungle sun, and everyone's asses were white as sheets. If Uncle Sam had seen us, I would have gotten a real skinning. According to the radio report, we were on a search-and-destroy mission.

One of the men said there were fish in the creek.

"Well, we've searched the area," I said. "Now let's destroy."

We found a deep hole and dropped a grenade in the water. Our mission was complete. We set up camp and cleaned the fish.

The average grunt platoon carried just about anything a person needed. Simmonds came through that day, and I would have put him in for a medal, but the Army never would have understood. He had a skillet which he'd never used in the bush, but he'd hung onto it faithfully. He also had some pancake mix which we rolled the fish in. I'd never seen fish like them, but they were the best tasting I'd ever had. Even the burnt part tasted better than anything I'd eaten since entering the country.

We'd not only sought and destroyed, but we'd eaten of the fruits of war, and all that had been wasted was one pineapple grenade. I thought that it would make up for a little of the toilet paper wasted by the career men.

I was sure that if I'd rolled fish in pancake mix and fried it that way back home, it would have tasted unbearable, but I can still taste the fish that we had that day in the jungle in Vietnam.

The only casualties we had were some bruises from hitting rocks with bare hide. No Purple Hearts were issued.

Not one enemy was seen by the Third, 187th, on that twenty-one-day stretch, so the colonel had been right. They were regrouping. I thought we had it made if the rest of the tour was going to be similar.

On the twenty-first day, we returned to Evans for three days. I had received a lot of mail. There was a tape from my brother, Roy, and a disturbing letter from my wife. She hadn't heard from me in three weeks, yet everyone else had. I couldn't understand it because I'd written faithfully at least once a week, and sometimes three or four times. I wrote a quick letter explaining it to her and mailed it personally.

Then I listened to Roy's tape, and it was a dandy. He'd had a college party and several girls had spoken to us. I took it over to the platoon and gathered them around to listen.

Roy's voice explained the party and then introduced the girls. In fun, the first girl asked, "Are you boys horny?" and Kotewa yelled, "Boys? There ain't no boys in Vietnam!" Each girl made a few comments to all of us. Two of them were Oriental.

Now, at another time and another place, we probably would have laughed until our sides hurt, but calling us boys only produced a low chuckle. So we took that tape and filled in some appropriate comments and sent it back to Roy.

I told him to have another party and not to play the tape until everyone was present. When the girl asked, "Are you a boys horny?" we broke in and said, "If you see a boy in Vietnam, jump on him and suck his dick." We felt like we had a masterpiece. I don't think Roy let the Orientals listen to it, but the others got a kick out of it.

I received a new replacement in May—a man by the name of Scarborough. After a few days in the field, he wanted out. He was a good man and I hated to lose him, but he couldn't stand the pressure. He wasn't a drinker or a smoker and everything upset him. I told him the best I could do was to get him a job with the captain, which normally was a safe position, but other than that, I couldn't promise anything.

One of the RTOs went home and I recommended Scarborough, and he got the job. I hated to recommend a new man over some of the men, but most of them didn't want to be with the captain anyway, so no one got upset with me; in fact, some felt I'd done the man an injustice.

11

During the three-day stand-down, I watched a couple of war movies, played bridge with the colonel, drank my share of free beer, and tried to relax.

May was coming to a close. I was supposed to go on R-and-R to Hawaii to see my wife, and I was counting the days. I had been in-country almost five months and it felt like ten years.

On the third day, I found out that my R-and-R was set for June 14-19. All the arrangements had been made with my wife. Mike and I talked about home and spent a lot of time together.

Mike was a junior in college at Bridgeport, Connecticut, when he decided to quit and get married. He knew he'd be drafted because of his age, so he chose to enlist. I'm not sure whether he wanted to go to OCS or if he just ended up there like me, but I think he wanted it because Mike was an achiever and liked a challenge.

I was twenty-three when I got drafted. I was older than my lieutenant in basic training and most of the drill sergeants, so I was called the old man. Mike called me this as well, so I nicknamed him Emmett for the last survivor of the Dalton Gang. First Platoon, of course, became the Dalton Gang. If we ever needed to talk personally, we agreed to use our nicknames over a clear channel on the radio where we could encourage each other.

Mike was just a year younger than I was, so he was an old man also. I'd received my promotion to first lieutenant while on the Razorback, and for two weeks I was Mike's senior officer. During those two weeks, we only met twice and while under battle conditions. Both times, Mike saluted and said, "At your direction, old man, sir!" My admiration for Mike was growing each day. He had a good rapport with his men and was well liked by everybody. His R-and-R was set for a week after mine. He was going to see his baby boy for the first time.

In our briefing, we were told we would be working an area that was close to the flats. We were to replace Bravo Company, and it had seen no action, so things looked pretty good.

At 0600 hours, we were on the helipad ready to go back to the field. A call came in telling us that several dinks had walked into one of our ambushes. My platoon was fresh and ready so we went to the scene and found that approximately twenty-five dinks had stumbled into a squad-sized ambush. Since it was on the flats, our squad could see the dinks coming. When their mechanical went off, they opened fire and killed and wounded several more. The squad was really happy when we arrived. No friendlies had been killed and they were high. There were ten dead enemies and plenty of blood trails to follow.

While I was talking to the squad leader, a full-bird colonel came out in a chopper with some reporters. They looked the dead over and took several pictures. Some of the squad put their feet on the dead dinks and had their pictures taken. I didn't know what a dead enemy was supposed to look like in the movies, but in the real world it wasn't a pretty sight.

Their uniforms were ragged and their shoes were anything from thongs to tennis shoes to no shoes at all. Only six of the men were carrying rifles. There was one dead woman and her grotesque black teeth were sickening to look at.

Again I wondered why we couldn't win the war. The enemy

was in rags and had no weapons. We had so much firepower, yet they fought on and on.

Apparently the enemy had been in the village all night and were returning to the hills with a few pounds of rice when they walked into the ambush. After the picture-taking, everyone left, including the squad from Bravo Company. We cleaned up the mess and sent the bodies and weapons somewhere. I supposed someone else wanted to see the dead. At least we didn't have to bury them.

I requested a dog team, and they sent me a booby-trap dog when I needed a personnel dog. We started out on a blood trail and found two more dead about one hundred meters from the ambush. I took a squad and followed another blood trail most of the day. We finally came to the first ridgeline, and by then our adrenaline was pumping full force.

When we hit the jungle, we found a large trail cut into the bush following a low ridge. It couldn't be seen from the air. After about one hundred meters of inching down the trail, I had had enough, and we returned to the platoon.

We set up our NDP and two ambushes that night. One was close to the trail, the other about two hundred meters away. Later, we heard the dinks, but they rerouted around us. It was our first night in the flats and I felt naked. There were no trees, no hills, just prairie. Every one hundred meters or so was a swampy area infested with snakes and leeches. We could see quite far during the day, but only a short distance at night.

I reported everything except the trail we had found. Along the Rockpile and Razorback, these trails were common. The next day I had plans to move closer to the trail and set up my ambushes. I figured if I had reported after dark, they might have decided I should move there in the dark and set up, so I failed to report it.

The fox reports ranged from three to ten that night. My faith in those reports was diminishing by the day. There were too many people waiting to find something, and some were willing to make up the enemy. Sometimes I wondered if some pilots didn't fly over and see us and send in an enemy report just for fun. I doubted that it was true, but it sure would have been a cruel joke if it were true.

The next morning, we sent the dog team back and reconned the trail. I wasn't sure what the military books said about going up a hill for the first time, but I felt that our weakest time was traveling up a new hill. If a person was on top shooting down, his accuracy was much greater than being on the bottom shooting up. And if he started on top, his rear guard could protect him from someone cutting him off.

The trail ran between two ridgelines, which meant the dinks could get above us in two areas and fire down at us like we were cattle. I decided to recon more of the area and pretend that the trail didn't exist for the time being.

For the next two weeks, we worked all around that trail, setting up night ambushes with no results. We suspected the enemy to be close almost every night, but they would always detour just before they walked into our ambushes. Even though we saw nothing, I knew we were being watched daily. Several times I debated whether to leave three men at the ambush site by the trail. I was sure we could have killed a few more dinks that way. A ten-man squad could set up the ambush and then seven men would leave at daylight. When we were followed, the three men would get some action.

The only fallacy was that the enemy seemed to know where our ambushes were set. I figured they were pretty dumb, but even a dink could count to ten and subtract three, and if he could, the three men were as good as dead. It wasn't worth the lives of three men to find out. Yet, after ten days of recon, we had not found any other trails or signs for several klicks.

Again I wished for a company of seventy-five to one hundred men. We could have shut down their supply line indefinitely. I was sure that other platoons had seen the same trail and that other lieutenants had thought the same thing. But the trail was an old one and heavily used. It was simply a case where air mobile units didn't spend enough time in any one place.

We were everywhere in Vietnam, yet we were nowhere. All the enemy had to do was wait a few days and one outfit would move out and another would move in. Each unit was doing its own thing. When we left the area, we didn't brief the incoming people. Everything went through the radio back to the rear area and then returned to the people in the field.

I always felt that even an hour with a new outfit would have been beneficial to the war effort. Had I been able to explain our every move and ambush tactics, the next outfit could have carried on. But anytime a unit became predictable to the enemy, it was in great danger. And we were very predictable.

As a general rule, the enemy tried to avoid contact with infantry squads because of our firepower and all the help we could have in a few minutes. However, if an American unit was lazy or asleep, the enemy would gladly knock off a few GIs and then *"di di moi"* into the jungle. Knowing this, I tried to be as unpredictable as possible.

As long as Sergeant Cuevas was around, he would keep the men awake, and as a result, our enemy contact was cut down considerably. Many night, old Charlie would probe the perimeter, but each time he found someone alert and ready for action. I never hesitated to fire artillery at anything the least bit suspicious.

By June 5, we had covered every inch along the first ridgeline, and that one trail was still the only fresh sign. Each day we probed it a little deeper, finding more signs from the night before. If we placed a mechanical ambush, they would walk around it. It was very unnerving to realize that every step we took was being watched, and yet we could see nothing.

Alpha Company was three klicks to our north, and one recon platoon was taking resupply. Fifteen men were ambushed. One man was killed and fourteen were wounded. All were serious enough for a ticket home. I wasn't there to know for sure, but I suspected that no one was pulling security since all fifteen men were wounded. Everyone had been too busy unloading mail and food from the choppers.

There was another example of poor strategy. Our platoons were down to squad-sized elements, yet we were to act as platoons. Had Alpha's platoon been forty-five instead of fifteen, someone would have been alert and had security out. Each platoon should have had at least three twelve-man squads. Instead, most of us had two seven-man squads, a lieutenant, medic, platoon sergeant, and RTO if we were lucky.

Several of the platoons had SP-4 squad leaders instead of sergeants. I was fortunate in having Sergeant Hill and Sergeant Gustafson, both E-5s. Although I could muster only two small squads, at least I had sergeants. I also had a few men who should have been sergeants, but the paper work had not come through.

Only three or four choppers were needed to airlift us in and out of the jungle when nine should have been required. When we were on stand-down, most of the lieutenants and sergeants complained of their men not wanting to pull security, except in known bad areas. They were also falling asleep on guard. Both Mike and I were extremely fortunate to have conscientious men in our platoons.

On the fifth of June, we were airlifted back to Evans for an early stand-down. It turned out that Captain Edwards was going home.

Lieutenant Harper, a West Pointer, had made captain and was to be our new CO. He would take over on the eighth when we returned to the field.

For three days, we drank our share again and prepared to return to the field. Mike and I spent a lot of time together. He had received pictures of his new baby and he was as proud as could be.

On the second night, Colonel Steverson came into the barracks and told me I was the senior lieutenant in the field.

"Sure, but Mike and about ten others are only a week behind me," I said.

"It doesn't matter," he answered. "Do you want a rear job?"

I had had a few whiskeys washed down with beer, and I quickly informed the colonel what he could do with his rear job.

A REMF's life was not for me; besides, only goof-off lieutenants got rear jobs. I didn't tell him how Colonel Sutton ran things, but it really upset me to be offered a REMF's job. I felt that I had done as well as any lieutenant in the field. The colonel felt a little perturbed at me.

Mike said I should have taken the offer.

"With only seven months left, you'd be assured of going home in one piece," he said incredulously.

"Sure," I replied. "But what about my seventeen men left in the field? I owe them something."

"Man, wake up. We got all kinds of new lieutenants just sitting around waiting to go to the bush."

"No way do I feel like a fuck-up. No way will I take that rear job," I said emphatically. "In fact, I'm going back to give the colonel a piece of my mind and find out what I've done wrong in the field to deserve a REMF's job.

It was the only time I saw the colonel's hootch. It was no different than ours except it was just as big, and it was private.

I jumped the colonel straight out and asked him what I had done wrong.

"You've done absolutely nothing wrong," he said.

"Come on, Colonel. The only way a lieutenant gets a rear job is if he has screwed up in the field."

"Where did you get an idea like that?" he asked.

"Colonel Sutton wanted only the best in the field. And the goof-offs got rear jobs. I took charge of a platoon and we had no one hurt or wounded, except Wheeler. And I'm the only platoon that can say that."

"Now I see why you're so upset," the colonel said and

nodded. "Well, I'm not Colonel Sutton. And I'm losing several captains, with no replacements in sight. And I want a good lieutenant to fill in until some captains do show up. As to your ability—that's why I want you. And if you don't think you're good enough to fill a captain's shoes, then I don't want you."

We had a good laugh about our misunderstanding. Then, for the next two hours, Mike and I visited with the colonel about the battalion.

Colonel Steverson was extremely proud of our outfit and was pleased about the overall effort of the platoons in the field. Mike and I filled his head full of facts about the good old draftees fighting to make the career men look good. He was truly concerned about the welfare of the men and asked if we saw any problems. We told him about the slow promotions coming to some of the men and how our recommendations seemed to fall on deaf ears.

"When we put a man in for a medal, we seldom get a response from headquarters," I said. "Our supply is about as good as can be expected, considering we are on the end of the supply line. Now that Major Mailbags is gone, things are pretty good."

"I really had to pull strings to get rid of him," the colonel said.

I laughed and said that in another two or three weeks I might have gotten rid of him myself. The colonel didn't laugh, but said that several REMFs had made the same comment, and he wanted him gone before a killing happened.

Mike and I left Colonel Steverson, and I told Mike I was glad we had had our talk with the CO, that he was a man who understood his purpose as a battalion commander and yet had the compassion to understand the problems that came with the job. I suddenly realized I was sober and felt good inside. I knew I wouldn't take the rear job, but it was nice to know I was wanted and not hated by someone.

The night of June 7 was a short one because Mike and I and several other lieutenants talked until about 3 A.M. There was a shortage of everything but lieutenants. When I'd been in boot camp at Fort Campbell, Kentucky, they were almost begging people to sign up for Officer Candidate School because of an extreme shortage of lieutenants. In Vietnam, we all sat around wishing we had PFCs to get back to strength, but the only replacements were lieutenants. It would have taken almost a company of men to make a full-sized platoon.

Mike's platoon had twenty-one men at the time, Lieutenant Johnson's had nineteen, and I had seventeen. That was a total of fifty-seven men in three grunt platoons when I had been taught that 135 grunts were required to fill out three platoons. I hoped, before I went to sleep, that none of the lieutenants were itching to get to the field over my dead body.

One new lieutenant who had been stationed in Hawaii was a really straight troop. He was going to take over the headquarter's company of REMFs. He said he would straighten them out and make them military. Johnson told him if he made them shine their boots he might not see the sun come up again. The new lieutenant talked big about how they would appreciate a little discipline and order.

"Has he ever got a surprise in store for him," I said.

At 0600, the whole company was on the helipad. It was Captain Edward's last day, June 8, 1971. We all landed on the same hill on the first ridgeline north and west of Camp Evans. Off to the west and a little south was Firebase Rakkasan, our namesake.

Our hill had been cleared by fire bombs. Some kind of fuel was mixed up with something else to make a jelly and it was placed in fifty-gallon drums. These detonated on impact and literally blew and burned a hole in the jungle. They made nice LZs, but everything was burned and smelled like fuel oil. A man came up looking black from just walking in it. It was not new to us so we dug in, smell and all. At least we didn't have to worry about insects and leeches for a few hours.

It was our first full-sized company operation. We had been

close before, but not everyone had been at the exact spot. After looking over my map, I realized that the trail which had been bugging us for so long was in the same area, probably down at the bottom of the hill.

I told Captain Edwards about it and he said, "Nobody leaves the perimeter for twenty-four hours." He was too short to be left alone. We would all be sitting tight for the night. When he got on that freedom bird, we could do anything we liked, but until then he wanted all the protection he could get.

This was not abnormal. Many men, when they got short, were leery about one last operation. It was always a worry to the platoon leaders. If a man was asked to go on recon, he would simply refuse, saying, "Send someone else. I'm too short."

So we constantly had to keep track of the short-timers. Some would accidentally sprain an ankle so they could go to the rear for a couple of days. I guessed that at any given time there were fifteen to twenty short-timers walking around the rear area trying to REMF their last two weeks. It was very understandable because too many GIs got hurt, not only by the dinks, but also by cherries and accidents.

The next morning at 0800, Captain Edwards left us to go home and Captain Harper took over. He had been a lieutenant in the field just two weeks before. Judging by the little I'd been around him as a lieutenant, he seemed like a good man. He immediately called all the lieutenants together. The speech was not one that I wanted to hear.

He said that Delta Company had been setting long enough and it was time for some action. He wanted body count and told us we could start right away. That was the career soldier in him talking, and I was sure he was a little nervous on his first day as a commander of Delta Company. He tried to lay out our mission in detail, our every step and our every communication.

"Captain," I said, "you give me a mission and my men will do it. But at our own pace and our own risk. No way could

I work under your conditions. ... When I leave this hill on recon, it will be like always."

Mike agreed wholeheartedly with me.

"Captain, you led a platoon," he said. "So give us some slack. You can trust us. We will complete the mission."

"Okay, gentlemen," Captain Harper said. "Just so we understand each other. Get your platoons ready to go. Lieutenant Johnson will stay with the CP. And you two will go on recon in the designated areas."

He indicated Mike and me.

Fate had a way of causing one to do things that under normal circumstances he would avoid. I volunteered to take Second Platoon down the east slope and intersect the trail. At least I would be on the top, going down. Mike said he would take First Platoon down the west slope and see if he could intersect the same trail. If we were both successful, then we would ambush the trail that night in two different locations.

I don't know to this day why I volunteered to go east instead of west. I thought I had chosen the worst direction. I knew that dink highway was down there and that we would find enemy activity before the day was over. Whether friendship with Mike caused me to take what looked to be the most dangerous route, or pure ignorance, I just don't know.

About sixty long days earlier, Mike and I had agreed to carry two grenades on our chests, so if we walked into a bad booby trap there would be no doubt of our outcome. We both agreed to go home in one piece or hundreds of pieces, but not crippled.

Just before leaving, Mike and I shook hands and told each other good luck and I said, "Be careful, man, because somewhere close is a bunch of dinks, and we're knocking at their front door."

"If I don't see you before the fourteenth," he said, "say hello to your wife for me."

"Give your kid a hug for me 'cause you'll be leaving about the time I get back." I answered.

Second Platoon left the hill first; then the Dalton Gang left a few minutes later. We hadn't been gone an hour when we found the trail. We carefully secured a small area and I called Mike. I told him the trail was curving around the hill toward his platoon.

We sat tight while Mike called the CO and reported finding the trail and a few used bunkers. The captain told him to take his time and check it out.

For the next two hours, First Platoon reported all kinds of caches. One cave-like bunker contained medical supplies.

"Be careful, man," I yelled. "Watch for booby traps!"

"An inch at a time, man," was his reply. "An inch at a time."

About five minutes later we heard a large explosion with two smaller ones right behind it. Mike's radio went dead. I sat down heavily and my heart stood still.

I knew immediately that Mike was dead. I didn't have to guess or wonder; I just knew. The two smaller explosions had to have been the hand grenades on his chest.

Mike was going home, just like we had agreed.

We sat and listened to the medevacs come in over our heads to pick up the bodies. There were four dead and two slightly wounded. They had checked out a trail leading to the medical bunker and it had appeared to be clean. In fact, they had made two trips over trail and carried contraband out of the bunkers.

On the third trip, Mike, or one man close to him, had stepped on a command-detonated mine. It had been a large shell, at least an 82mm mortar round, if not bigger. Its killing radius was thirty-five meters. It alone would have killed the four men. The man that stepped on it must have literally been blown to pieces.

A squad from Third Platoon left the hill to help the remainder of First Platoon. There wasn't enough of Mike left that was recognizable as a man. All that was left was pulp. The other three men were also killed instantly.

We just sat around dumbfounded. The idea of being ten thousand miles away from home didn't make sense to me. It was all unthinkable. We could have been ambushed ourselves right then. It just didn't seem to matter anymore.

"Get back to the top of the hill immediately," the captain's voice crackled over the radio.

"On the way," I replied.

But we just sat staring at the ground. After about an hour, the CO asked for our location.

"ETA about fifteen minutes," I answered. Every step back was agony. My thoughts were concentrated on Mike and his men. He had been as good and careful as any man could be. I know he had checked the area inch by inch. But those God-forsaken booby traps defied all reasoning. No one could escape their terror. No modern technology could help us against them.

There were no John Wayne types. Some men had a sixth sense part of the time, but nobody could walk the jungle for twelve months and expect to avoid all the booby traps. Some had been placed years before and were still effective. The jungle grew quickly, and after a few days, all signs were covered up. Only an extra sense could help a man in those cases, and he couldn't stand the pressure every day. Some of the old booby traps even killed a few dinks. Our only safety lay in cutting new trails and hoping the old booby traps were useless.

We reached the top the hill. The rest of Mike's men, fifteen of them, were sitting staring into space. Shock had set in on their faces.

Captain Harper said they'd call an air strike if they could get proper coordinates. I told him to give them the whole valley and tell them to blow it to bits until there was nothing left standing. The colonel flew over and dropped a red smoke on the target. Seven different smokes appeared; five reds, one yellow, and one violet.

The colonel landed and we handed him some flares, hoping

the enemy didn't have any. He flew over again and dropped his flares, and eleven different smoke grenades came wafting up from all over the valley. There was no doubt that the valley contained a large number of the enemy.

"After all these years, the enemy is still living within rifle shot of us," I told Captain Harper, "and no one has disrupted their procedures."

They sent choppers out to airlift us off the ridgeline. As we were leaving, we could see different colors of smoke still rising out of the jungle. The artillery was starting to fire HE. I wanted to stay in the bird and watch the whole valley being blown away.

The area had been worked for years. Firebase Rakkasan was on the south end of the valley, and Firebase Jack was only five miles into the flats. One of the red smoke grenades was billowing its smoke only three hundred meters from Firebase Rakkasan.

We had lost four good men and all we could do was spend a million dollars killing a few trees and bushes while the enemy went underground. Only a direct hit on a bunker (or spider hole) would kill the dinks. Nonetheless, I suspected that we tightened a few assholes that day and maybe even killed a few of them. I hoped that we'd destroyed enough terrain to set them back a few months to recover and rebuild, if nothing else.

12

We flew south of Rakkasan and landed on another ridgeline further west into the jungle. The LZ was cold and secure when we landed. I took seven of Mike's men with the platoon and went on a recon. I didn't push anyone, especially the members of First Platoon. For all purposes, they were just there for a while and were of little use. The heat and the humping that afternoon helped take the edge off the situation.

We found a small stream about 4 P.M. and set up for night. There was no sign of the enemy anywhere, so we relaxed a little. We all washed in the clear stream water. Some shaved. Some wrote letters home. I was devastated inside and began to wonder what I was doing and who I was. My platoon was down to fifteen men and I still had no replacements. I didn't know nine of them very well.

I sat down and opened a letter from home and tried to read it, but nothing seemed to help. I placed the letter in my pocket to finish later. I told Irons I was going to take a walk into the jungle and that I'd be back in a little while. I walked out about fifty yards and sat down with my weapon across my knees and cried like a baby.

After a while, a calmness settled over me like nothing I'd felt before. I thought about home. I'd been raised on a dairy farm in central Illinois. It was thirty miles to a town of any size and five miles to the nearest town. From the time I was five years old I was packing a gun and hunting close to home. The old Daisy pump BB guns had enough power to kill blackbirds and swallows. I'd enjoyed those early years, and once in a while I'd gotten lucky and had hit a squirrel or rabbit in the head and really brought home the bacon.

At age ten, I carried an old single-shot .410 gauge, and from that point on, I had to have a hunting coat to carry all the game. When I wasn't in the woods, I was fishing for yellow-bellied catfish in the old pond. I didn't have a worry in the world then. Sometimes I thought I did, but those were the golden years. The work was hard, but Dad was fair, and it seemed like I had plenty of time for both work and play.

Then my eyes focused on the jungle brush again and I found

myself ten thousand miles from home. The lives of the men in my platoon weighed heavily on my shoulders. It was difficult for me to conceive of glory and country when we seemed to be gaining nothing. Our casualty figures rose higher and higher every day, yet we didn't accomplish anything.

We knew that the dinks were back in their bunkers laughing at us, writing home about killing four more stupid Americans. They were living in the valleys and we were living on the ridgelines, and neither side cared for open battle. Search-and-destroy was our game, and yet, as soon as we destroyed something, the NVA would start it all over again. They had been there for years. We found one enemy KIA who had letters to that effect. He had been in Quang Tri province for six years and knew every cave, hole, trail, and booby trap for miles around.

Each of us was there for twelve months and then we were rotated home. Even our battalion commanders served twelve months. There was only a small percentage of soldiers who were on their second tour.

The jungle wasn't good for anything. It was nothing like the woods back home with all its smells and flowers. The heat was a real killer. We each carried a hundred pounds, and the dinks carried about ten at the most.

It was four days until I would go to Hawaii, but I didn't want to go. I hated the jungle, yet was drawn to it. I'd been in the bush only five months, but I felt like it was all that I knew. Home and family were things I could no longer comprehend. There was no way I could go home and hunt and fish as I used to. And there was no way my family could understand a grunt's feeling. I knew then how those young men who had been here felt. With the bad publicity and the uprooted feeling of being torn from the home folk, I knew it was going to be rough going home.

I decided then that I would take the first rear job offered. No friends would die because I had made a mistake. I longed for some kind of news about a victory or anything positive about the war, but somehow I knew there would be nothing. If the Americans pulled out the next day, the NVA would walk about a klick and own it all, anyway, and the ARVNs would collapse quickly.

With so few men in the field, it was easy to make a mistake. Everyone was taxed to the limit of endurance. Army perimeters became smaller and smaller. Night watch became longer and longer. It was only a matter of time before we would all be dead. I didn't mind dying at that point, but I knew what the feeling would be back home. I could hear my dad in the coffee shop after the initial grief: "My son died, and it was senseless, foolish, and all for nothing." And most everyone would agree with him.

Dying for nothing bothered me. Mike's death had been for nothing. We couldn't avenge it or justify it. Deep down I wanted to take the platoon and whip someone. But there was nothing I could do except get more men hurt in the process so more fathers would cry and the draft evaders could fuel the publicity fire.

I walked back to the platoon and ate supper and waited for dark. Everything was quiet for the next three days, and Mike's men gradually came out of their shells. We seemed to be working a pretty safe area.

On the twelfth of June, a bird showed up to take me to the rear. It was a weird feeling to lift off the ground and look down at the men, watching them get smaller and smaller, realizing that some or all could be dead by the time I got off R-and-R. I almost had the chopper turn around, but instead I felt that the men were as good without me as they were with me. Maybe a few days off would help.

When I got to the rear, I opened some new mail and found out that Marc McClellan from Martinsville, Illinois, was only fifty miles away at Phu Bai. I had a full day to waste getting there, so I took a jeep and drove it myself, hoping to catch

Marc on stand-down. I didn't figure I could catch him, but at least I'd be alone to think during the trip.

Driving fifty miles by jeep was like one hundred miles by car. After being on the road for twenty minutes, I realized that I was still in jungle fatigues and had my M-16 propped against my leg. I knew I couldn't go to Hawaii dressed like that, so when I got to Phu Bai I would have to find some clothes. The jeep belonged to Uncle Sam and I had temporarily borrowed it. I was upset, so I hadn't checked it out properly, but the ARVNs would get it someday anyhow, so I thought I had claim to it. I had a lot more time to think, and if Marc was there, I'd have some time to visit as well.

Marc's dad was a state trooper back home, and he had given me my first two tickets. He was a good man and was well respected. I didn't know Marc personally, but like all small towns, a person knew everyone a little.

I pulled into First of 501st and tramped into headquarters, rifle and all, and asked for Marc McClellan. The sergeant told me he'd been wounded about ten days earlier and had just gotten out of the hospital.

Five minutes later, Marc came in.

"Hello, Don," he said.

"McClellan, don't you know the proper way to greet an officer?" the sergeant asked.

"Back off, Sergeant," I responded. "We're hometown boys. Uncle Sam doesn't need our bodies every minute."

Marc was feeling good, but he was a little slow at moving. I told him I had all day if he did, and we went to the enlisted men's club for a beer. After a while, we just sort of stared at each other, and finally Marc asked, "How are we going to go home and tell anyone what Nam is really like?"

"No way, man," I answered. "We can only try."

Marc had been wounded while pulling security for a bulldozer. His squad had been completely overrun, and Marc had had a satchel charge go off behind him. It burned both his legs and threw dirt and pebbles into them. If it had been an American grenade, he would have been dead. His wounds were serious enough to have him sent home, but Uncle Sam hadn't seen it that way. Therefore, Marc had to suffer the heat and try to heal in-country.

We talked and drank for a couple of hours, and I found out his outfit was on 719 and had suffered as many casualties as Third, 187th. While in the hospital, he had heard that most of the battalions had lost several men.

Some of Marc's friends joined us and we got down to some serious drinking. By four in the afternoon, we were feeling pretty mellow when the CQ (charge of quarters) sergeant came over and told me that since he wasn't allowed in the officer's club, I shouldn't be allowed in the EM club.

"Back off, Sergeant," Marc said. "We aren't hurting anything."

But the sergeant was a lifer and he insisted.

"Sergeant," I said. "I don't give a shit what you want. I came to visit Marc and that's what I'm going to do."

"Marc ought to be in his bunk resting," the sergeant replied.

"Back off, Sergeant!" Marc was getting pissed. His buddies agreed and helped escort the sergeant to another table. He said he would get the colonel.

"Well, war is hell, Sergeant," Marc said.

"But contact is a motherfucker," I added. Everyone laughed except the sergeant. He left, I supposed, to get the colonel.

I had to catch a shit-hook for Da Nang at six o'clock, and the rest of the afternoon was a little fuzzy because of the beer, but the colonel never showed up, and, because of the mood we were in, it was a good thing. I was tired of protocol and happy to be with a man from my hometown again. A colonel couldn't have moved either one of us without some opposition. Being a grunt in a war zone had a stigma about it that caused non-grunts to push a little harder than normal.

When I boarded the shit-hook after saying goodbye to Marc, the boarding chief made me unload my M-16. I sat down in a webbed seat for a two-hour flight to Da Nang. Shit-hooks get the job done, but I don't recommend them to airlines as a regular means of transportation.

I checked in my weapon at Da Nang and talked a supply sergeant out of a pair of khaki pants and a shirt. Then I went to a real Army PX store and got all my insignia, but I still felt totally naked. Without the leech straps bound around my legs, the khaki pants felt like balloons hanging down from my waist. Without my M-16, I had both hands free. There were dinks everywhere at Da Nang, but I didn't know whether they were VC or not.

Several men from the first and second corps area were going on R-and-R, so they billeted us all together. I didn't talk to anyone except other grunts. It was easy to spot them because their clothes looked slept in and baggy. The REMFs and lifers were all straight, right down to their shoestrings.

Just before boarding our plane, I ran into a captain who was our artillery FO (forward observer) for the battalion. He was extremely good at his job, but he smoked a lot of grass and seemed to enjoy nudity. More than once, while on stand-down, he was found sunbathing in the nude, except for his steel pot. He was a joker and always talked a mile a minute. He told me he had spent the previous night with two Vietnamese girls in downtown Da Nang.

"Man, what if you get the clap and give it to your wife?" I asked.

"Nothing to worry about," he answered. "Those girls were clean."

We sat together on the plane. He was really weird, in my book. He did all the talking, mostly about sex and Mary Jane.

Several hours of sex talk later, we landed in Hawaii. When I got off the plane, I was shocked. After five and a half months in the bush, I had forgotten what civilization was like. The noise of so many people, the loudspeakers, the thousands of people dressed in expensive clothes—it all had me shell-shocked.

I finally found my wife, and we all went to a briefing room. We were told when to be back and were given a rundown on some interesting tours that were cheap for servicemen.

I was still uncomfortable. It was hard to describe my feelings. I was glad to see my wife, yet I was still in the jungle. It was almost like the Twilight Zone to me. I could see faces of the men I'd left behind and wondered how many were alive or wounded. I couldn't look at my wife and say, "Honey, let's boogie," when my strange surroundings made me uncomfortable.

We checked into a hotel and my wife bought out some civilian clothes—blue jeans and a tee shirt. I took a shower and it felt so good that I hated to shut off the water. It was as if I were dirty and just couldn't wash Vietnam off me. After putting on the jeans and shirt, I did come back to the real world some, but my mind was busy with thoughts of the platoon. There were so few of them left that one ambush could wipe them out. Luckily, my wife did not question me, but seemed to understand. My days and nights were backwards. I was used to short naps of one to three hours and I was very restless. My wife was tired from her long trip so we ate supper and went to bed. I tried to sleep, but the bed was so soft that I couldn't get comfortable. So I got up and took another shower.

I went down the street and found an all-night diner that served chicken. I ate a whole chicken under the stares of several people. As I was leaving, I walked by a cigarette machine which was full of all the popular brands. There wasn't a Pall Mall or Kent to be found. I thought that the guys in the bush smoked odd brands of cigarettes and the rest of the world, including the dinks, smoked the good ones. It just didn't seem right.

I returned to the hotel and lay down on the floor beside the bed and fell asleep. Just before daylight I woke up and crawled into bed, and this time I slept soundly for a couple of hours.

The entire R-and-R was a torment to me, and I was sure it wasn't what my wife had expected, either. A few years later, I couldn't remember what we did or where we went, except for one incident.

On the second night, we found a secluded bar with a one-man band. His name was Chuck Hamen. He sang country music and that was the only place I felt comfortable in. Listening to Chuck sing and play took me back home to rural Illinois. I was really consuming the beer when a bunch of Navy men came in and sat close to us. They were a little rowdy, but they left us alone.

When I drink a lot of beer, my bladder tends to go to work, so I was frequently going to the john, and the Navy guys were picking up on my wife each time I was gone. I knew something was going on by her face and Chuck's wife's face as well, but I didn't know exactly what was happening. The bartender was always staring at us when I looked his way. I was used to servicemen having a good time, so I didn't figure it out for a while.

Finally, I walked to the restroom and then looked around the corner, and sure enough, one of them hurried over to my wife. I quickly did my thing and returned to her and Mrs. Hamen. I asked my wife if they were bothering her, and she said no, but I could tell she was trying to hide the truth. She told me that the bartender was also the bouncer and that he was well qualified to handle the situation.

I went over to him and told him that if anyone laid a hand on my wife there would be hell to pay. I was on edge anyway, and a good fight might have helped, but there were four of them and only one of me. But Dad had always said, "When you're right, stand up for it." I thought that if they wanted a fight, I would oblige, and the newspaper could report another Nam vet crazy for wrecking a bar.

They finally left, and I was glad because my bladder was needing a little drain and I wasn't going to leave my wife alone again. The bartender came over and gave us all free drinks and thanked me for not starting anything.

Outside of my wife and I rediscovering the finer art of sex, there wasn't much to remember about Hawaii. Ten showers a day, fried chicken every day, and sex. Well, I guess I remembered some things after all, but I was never really comfortable the whole time. I knew when I boarded the plane that I owed my wife a return trip to Hawaii some day. But there was no way she could have understood my feelings then, or even now.

On the return plane, I sat down beside the artillery captain once again. He was lighting up a Mary Jane cigarette while the no smoking sign was on. The stewardess told him to put it out.

"What are you going to do if I don't?" he asked.

"Kick you off the plane," was her reply.

"Go ahead," he told her. "Anything beats going to Nam."

She realized her mistake, and by then several of us had lit cigarettes, so she just went back to her seat and buckled up for the flight.

We landed at Da Nang, and I went for my jungle clothes. The supply sergeant offered me a new set, and I finally found a pair to suit me. I dug out my old leech straps and tied them on. He asked me what they were for and I told him.

"It ain't that bad, is it, Lieutenant?"

"When you can stand in one spot and watch literally hundreds crawling toward you, it's that bad," I answered. "They're about an inch long and as big around as a pencil led ... until they're full of blood. Then they get fat like the pencil itself. You can stand in one spot and make like you're moving in one direction, and they'll all turn toward you at once, like they have some radar sense or something."

He returned my rifle and ammo. I started to load it and thought better of it.

When the shit-hook landed at Phu Bai, I found the jeep minus its spare tire and headed back for Camp Evans and good old Rakkasan. When I got there, the company was on stand-down. I hurried to the area to find out what had happened. The platoon had seen no action. As I walked toward the barracks, I heard the familiar twang of a Jew's harp, and I knew John Sherman was still around.

When I entered, I saw Jim Stacy, Floyd Kotewa, Brent Burford, and Poncho all playing Spades. Floyd looked up.

"Did you get any mud for your turtle?" he asked me.

They all laughed and razzed me for a while.

"Good to have you back," Irons said. "Sergeant Cuevas is driving us all nuts."

Tex Lissenbee said I was to go to S-4 right away. I asked why and Dennis Davis smiled and said something about a shortage of compasses and maps.

"I got their compasses right here," Floyd said, pointing to his pecker.

Chief Warrant Officer Hall met me at S-4 and said, "You owe me eleven compasses."

"Man, I don't have them," I answered.

"I saw some of your men with them."

"Don't blame me," I told him. "I didn't sign any out."

"That's the problem. No one did. Besides, I need them for all the new lieutenants."

"Take it up with the colonel because I don't have any idea where your compasses are," I said.

I returned to the barracks and saw several of the men sitting around with compasses hanging around their necks. I told them that they were depriving a few lieutenants of having their very own GI compasses. Floyd grabbed his pecker and John twanged his Jew's harp. It was good to be back among friendly faces that understood.

"You guys better keep those hidden for a while 'cause the chief is pissed," I said. "And he knows some of you have them."

Tex then told me that Doc Wilson had a bad case of malaria and was on his way home via the hospital. Irish Wagner had been switched to a mortar platoon.

"Fourteen men in the field, and no medic," I mused aloud.

"Thirteen," Poncho Garcia said. "I'm too short to go back. ... Flint, Michigan, in ten days."

I couldn't believe my ears. In two days, I'd be going back to the bush with only thirteen men. What used to take seven or eight birds would only take three.

Our LZ was cold again, and we were on the first ridgeline. We had been close to that area before. Late on the third day, twenty-five dinks were spotted in the flats heading for the jungle and hills. I think every helicopter for twenty miles came in and fired-up the area. We watched from our hill, and all night long it looked like the Fourth of July. The next day, Charlie Company reconned the area and found absolutely nothing. The next morning, one of Charlie Company's mechanicals went off. They had killed an eight-year-old boy.

13

They were called Coke kids because they would walk from a village with a case of Cokes and sell them for a dollar apiece. Charlie Company hadn't retrieved their mechanical early enough and counted one enemy KIA. I classed the child as enemy because, for the next three days, VC from the village got revenge to the point where a tired Charlie Company had to be airlifted to a new area.

By June 20, I had a new medic, my first replacement in months. I was talking with him when Irons interrupted.

"Lieutenant," he said, "watch that other hill for a while and see if anything looks different."

It was dark, but the jungle was alive with fire flies or lightning bugs. I finally asked Irons what he'd seen. He pointed to a certain area and said the lightning bugs were moving downhill and getting closer to our ridgeline. A small light would come on then go off, and then a few feet farther down, it would flash on again. We watched it for about an hour and agreed that it wasn't normal. The light was too bright to be a lightning bug. I adjusted artillery for two hours up and down the side of the hill.

The next day, all fourteen of us went to check it out. We found a new trail with fresh cuttings, and at the end of the trail we also found our lightning bug. It was a D-cell battery with a flashlight bulb and a small wire wrapped around the bulb. By holding the bulb on one end of the battery and the wire on the other, the bulb would light. As the enemy walked, they would flash the light for an instant and take a couple of steps, then flash the light again. To an unconcerned eye, it would appear to be a lightning bug. We had gotten pretty close with the artillery or they wouldn't have dropped their light. We chalked one up for Kenny Irons and his alertness.

It was so hot that we spent the rest of the day just sitting around. I tried to write a letter home, but my sweat kept smearing the ink. I sat perfectly still in the shade and water ran off me. It was only about fifty yards to a stream, but it seemed about five miles in the heat.

That night, about 2:30 A.M., we heard noises. It sounded like enemy movement. We tightened our assholes and waited. They appeared to be moving past us. At one point, we blew a Claymore just to show them we were awake, and the range was close enough to have killed some of them.

Irons and I decided they were headed for the command post about five hundred meters away. We called the CO and informed him of our suspicions. Sure enough, about daylight they hit the CP and ran. They came by us running to beat the full rays of sunlight. We fired in their general direction, but, as usual, we could not confirm any dead or wounded. They always carried their dead with them whenever possible. No one had been hurt at the CP, and the entire fire fight had lasted about five minutes.

We spent the next few days reconning the area, but we found nothing. I figured the reason for the attack was because of Mike's find a few days earlier. There was no good reason for attacking a command post unless it was an act of revenge or because we were close to a cache. Since we hadn't found a cache, I figured it was revenge for tearing up their little hospital.

We settled for a few glimpses of the enemy, and several times we were fired upon by a lone dink. We called him Cackling Rosie because he would fire a short burst of automatic fire at us about three times a day. We never saw him. He must have been a poor shot or was simply shooting at the direction of our noises because he never came close to hitting us. His harassment kept us alert and wondering what we were close to.

Finally, on the last day before stand-down, we were back on the first ridgeline and relative safety. I was down to twelve men in the field. I was also spending my last night in the field and didn't know it.

When we reached Camp Evans, we were told that we were getting three days at Eagle Beach. Fun and sun for all. They loaded us on Chinooks, and Delta Company landed at the beach. We stacked our M-16s in connexes and placed our rucksacks in our hootches. We purchased swimming trunks and Hawaiian shirts at a small store. I also bought a cheap hat. My fair skin made me burn easily, so I spent a few extra dollars.

There was a Filipino band playing on an outdoor stage and also a small basketball pad made of cement. It turned out that our luck was bad because the tide was too rough to swim, so we spent the time drinking and listening to the band. I consumed my share of whiskey, and by noon I was pretty well soused.

The enlisted men and officers were separated by a thin wall. The only real advantage I saw for an officer was that there were fewer of us, so we could usually find a seat. Most of our officers were lieutenants and not lifers, so we had a good time together.

The chow hall was set up so that we could piece at about anytime, and meals were served military style—early breakfast, noon meal, and then early supper. The drinking went on continuously except for short meal breaks. By midnight the first night, I was so intoxicated that I fell into bed and missed breakfast.

There was no pressure at Eagle Beach; we could spend the time any way we wanted to. At noon the second day, they told us we had only two days and then it would be back to Evans. The platoon decided it should have one hell of a party. I went into the enlisted side of the bar, much to the dislike of a few lifers. Since there were only thirteen of us left, including myself, we were a closely knit group and didn't care who liked it. We alternated between the band and the bar. I'm not saying I was getting polluted again, but I played basketball barefooted on the cement and I didn't hurt my feet at all.

The bar closed about midnight and only seven of us were left drinking. The other pussies couldn't hold their booze and had fallen asleep somewhere. We seven each bought a case of beer and went to the beach to finish our party.

When we'd sat down in our little circle, I popped a top on the first beer, and I knew I wasn't going to make it any further. I started walking to the hootch and I remember falling down and crawling a little way, and then I either passed out or went to sleep in the sand.

I woke up the next morning in my bunk, and to this day I don't know how I got there, and no one has been able to tell me. There was sand in my eyes and it stuck to my eyebrows. It was everywhere, including the crack of my ass. I lay perfectly still for at least ten minutes, trying to decide if I was alive. I finally decided I was, and for another ten minutes I tried to decide if I wanted to be alive. If my mother could have seen me then!

My bladder reminded me that if I didn't do something quickly I was going to revert to infancy. It was a tough decision to make, but I decided that a good old country pee at the corner of the building would suffice because the latrine was at least ten yards away from the building.

As I leaned on the building and took a leak, I looked through my gritty eyes at the beach. On my high school senior trip, we had watched a new movie called *Lawrence of Arabia*. One scene showed dead men lying in the sand. We could have saved them a lot of money during the filming because the beach was full bodies in every position imaginable.

A couple of REMFs walked by, and I was still draining the old lizard. "Use the latrine like civilized people," one of them said.

I shook my little red pecker at them and said, "I got your latrine right here."

I shook the sand out of my poncho liner and crashed back to sleep. At about ten o'clock, a sergeant woke me and said, "Two hours 'til liftoff." I felt a little better so I got up and took a shower.

As long as I didn't touch my head, the rest of my body seemed to be functioning okay. I drank some tomato juice for breakfast and found Sergeant Cuevas.

"Hour-and-a-half 'til lift-off," I said in a low tone. "Get the men ready."

We started looking for the men. They were scattered everywhere. A couple were asleep on the beach, still hugging their cases of beer. By then the sun was hotter than hobilly hell, but they didn't notice.

At liftoff time, we got our weapons and rucks, and I swore mine weighed four hundred pounds. I asked Cuevas if everyone was accounted for, and he wasn't sure if he even knew how many there were supposed to be. We laid our rucks down and went to sleep immediately. The noise of the shit-hook couldn't keep us awake. Just before I fell deeper into sleep I heard Tex say, "War is hell," and someone else answered, "But Eagle Beach is a motherfucker."

Back at Evans we all skipped dinner and tried to recuperate. I tried to eat something at supper to settle my churning innards. Surprisingly, it helped a bunch, and I felt better.

As I was walking back to the company area, the colonel stopped me. "You've got a rear job and won't be going back to the field," he told me.

It was 3 July, and I'd been in the bush for six months.

"I can't desert them now," I said.

"My decision is final," he answered. "Besides, there are a new bunch of cherries who have just signed in. The platoon will get six new men and a new lieutenant. And more are expected soon."

I returned to D Company and told the men that I was a REMF and would introduce them to their new lieutenant. I could see desertion written all over their faces. We were a good team and didn't want to be broken up. I told them that I'd tried to turn it down, but that the colonel wouldn't let me.

I left and went to my bunk, and if I'd have been alone, I would have cried, but several lieutenants were there, one of whom was my replacement, Lieutenant Joy. He seemed like a nice guy and I decided he would be all right. He wasn't cocky and was willing to listen while I explained the small platoon to him. The next day, the platoon left for the field and I was lost in the rear area.

I went to the colonel's office and he dropped another bombshell on me. The battalion was going to move 350 miles south to pull security for the 173rd while they went home. I was to take over S-4 and would be in charge of the move.

"The only thing I know about supply is that it's where to go to get things and sign your name," I said.

"Chief Warrant Officer Hall is experienced and capable," the colonel assured me. "So listen to him and things will work out. We won't be leaving until late July, so you've got time to prepare. Now go start learning."

I carried my ruck and rifle into the S-4 hootch and shook hands with Chief Warrant Officer Hall.

"Here I am, Chief, a lieutenant filling a captain's shoes," I said. "I know absolutely nothing, so teach me. I won't bullshit you if you won't bullshit me. You run it and I'll help you all I can, but whatever you say goes."

"That's fine, until you learn," he said. "But I'm going home in late August, so you'd better learn quickly and hope for an experienced captain to come along."

For the next three weeks, I was so busy learning the supply business and the REMF life that the time flew by. I checked on the platoon every day, and all seemed to be going well without me. I was on the other end of the supply; instead of sending a resupply list, I was receiving one. I had come to the conclusion that the resupply REMFs were lazy and no good, but I was quickly changing my mind. Taking care of a battalion in the field meant almost daily resupply to some unit.

And every day there was a request that could not be filled. The only things we weren't short of were C-rations and ammunition. We had to watch everything else like hawks or else it disappeared. There were always requests for ice and chain saws, both of which we didn't have. I knew the needs of the bush babies because I had come from there, and I told the chief that I was going to do my best to fill all requests before I left. He wished me good luck, but told me things were scarce as hens' teeth.

We had a young man by the name of Tom Wooldridge who was a sharp individual, and he and I hit it off immediately. Everyday he checked out a jeep, and we drove around all units in Evans trying to acquire things for the troops.

I had a battalion to move and I didn't have the slightest

idea how I was going to do it. The Air Force was to move us, so I went to the liaison office and found out that C-130s were going to be used. I got all the information as to how much one plane would carry, and Tom and I started back to Rakkasan.

We passed an ice house, so we turned around and went back. It was run by a sergeant and a few dinks from the village. The ice wasn't fit to put in GIs' drinks because it wasn't pure enough, but the dinks grew up on it and didn't mind the dirty-looking blocks.

The sergeant explained that they made ice in six-foot-by-eight-inch-by-six-inch blocks for the civilian hospital and villages. I asked what it would take to get a few blocks daily for the battalion. He informed me that it couldn't be done and that it wasn't fit for American consumption. I told him that the men wouldn't drink it, but would ice down their beer and pop in the field. He laughed and said that a block would only last about four hours in the heat.

"It wouldn't hurt to try," I said. But he gave me the old military strategy that it was unauthorized and he could get in deep trouble if he got caught. I offered him whiskey and C-rations.

"I get hot meals three times a day," he said. "What would I do with C-rations?"

"Give them to the slopeheads to keep their mouths shut about the ice," I told him.

We finally agreed on two captured AK-47 rifles, two quarts of whiskey, and a daily case of C-rations. When I told Chief Hall about my good fortune, he gave me the "I-can't-believe-you" look that told me I was crazy.

But the next day's supply went out with four blocks of ice. The CO of Charlie Company was ecstatic, and he called me personally to thank me. There were still a lot of shortages, but things could only be accomplished one at a time.

Making the move to Cam Ranh Bay took almost three-quarters of my time. We finally figured that by loading the C-

130s to their maximums, it would take nine planes to move the entire battalion: four birds to move the troops and five more to move all of our equipment.

It was hectic, and I was catching it from all sides. Some of the COs were crawling my ass everyday about resupply. There was nothing I could do but take it. There was only so much supply available, and we were too far north to get the best stuff anyway, so all I could do was try my best and let the complaints go sliding off my shoulders as easily as possible. Since I had been a bush baby, I couldn't hate a captain for trying to shake up the REMFs and get all he could for his men. Thank God, July was about over, and I could count the remaining months on one hand.

Camp Evans was almost as far north as a person could get in Vietnam and still be in the infantry. Cam Ranh Bay was 350 miles south and on the ocean, and it was not a free-fire zone. The Air Force and Navy were also stationed there, so the Third of 187th was going to civilization compared to the hills of I Corps Area.

Each day, as I worked on the move, I felt pulled toward the hills and guilty that I was in the rear area. Those ridgelines kept beckoning. I couldn't shake the feeling that I had somehow deserted my men. I wasn't a career officer, but I had a career position. I kept complaining to the CO to get me back in the bush, but he never understood. He told me to keep up the good work and all would work out. It was seven more days to Cam Ranh Bay, and I thought that after the move I might feel different. At least those ridgelines wouldn't be staring at me every morning.

I kept in touch with Kenny Irons and Tex Lissenbee, as well as most of the twelve whom I'd known so well. Brent Burford had been bitten by a rat and was in the rear taking his twenty-one shots in the belly—one shot each day. He suffered a lot, and I hoped that nothing that had teeth would bite me while I slept. I didn't relish the thought of taking those shots. I doubted if any man spent a full twelve months in the bush without something or someone getting to him. I had been fortunate in my time, but so had Burford. I knew if I had stayed in the bush that fatigue, if nothing else, would have gotten to me.

The last two days at Camp Evans were spent getting everything to the airstrip and into nine separate loads. I had a plan that Westmoreland would have been proud of, if he could have seen it. The colonel's jeep was to go in the first bird, along with an advance guard and some of my S-4 people. The CO would go on the second bird, and his jeep and driver were to be waiting for him when he landed. The rest of the birds would haul connexes full of supplies, and the men would fill in the spaces.

The first bird finally landed and we were ready. As we were loading, I got my first lesson from the Air Force, and it was one I didn't like. The air crew was supervising the loading when a pilot, a lieutenant colonel, came up and told me he couldn't take everything I'd planned. I told him we'd weighed everything and that it was within the Air Force guidelines for a C-130. He told me he didn't give a damn what the guidelines said; he was in charge, and nobody could make him take more than he wanted. He said he'd take everything but the jeep. I was arguing with him when my CO came up. Colonel Steverson inquired about the problem, and I explained, so he went a few rounds with the Air Force lieutenant colonel and the Air Force won.

He took off and the second bird landed. This time an Air Force major looked over his load and said, "Fine. I'll take it all."

I felt a little better, but I was still short room for the CO's jeep. The third bird refused some of its cargo. I was beginning to learn about the Air Force. As the fourth bird landed, I rushed twenty-five extra men over to his load and he took them all. I did the same on the fifth and sixth birds. This made room for the colonel's jeep on the seventh load.

When the ninth bird landed, I had a full load plus about eleven men, including myself. The pilot wasn't very happy about the load, but since he was last, he finally agreed to take it. I wasn't sure of all the chances I was taking by overloading some birds, but we made it to Cam Ranh Bay in the nine loads, some heavy and some light. Outside of the colonel not having his jeep for two hours, everything else went smoothly.

After we landed in the last bird, we used deuce-and-a-half trucks to haul everything to our new home. Compared to Evans, it had far nicer facilities than we'd been used to. The compound was on a slight hill and was compact in nature. All the hootches were a lot closer together than at Evans. The S-4 supply area had a concrete floor and plenty of storage. It definitely took my mind off the jungle because it was so hectic for the following three days that I wasn't sure how we managed.

Everyone in S-4 had had very little sleep. However, most of the grunts were packed with supplies and ready to go, which was a blessing amidst a nightmare. Our radio contact was all new and it was like starting all over again from scratch. The S-4 driver, Tom Wooldridge, and I spent most of our time learning where everything was and how to get it for the men.

The first two weeks were sheer hell because no matter how hard we worked and how many hours we spent, someone always needed something ASAP, and the war effort was lost if S-4 didn't get it immediately. Somehow the REMFs managed to pull through, and we accomplished our job with what I would like to think was an excellent, expedient manner. It probably depended on whom a person asked, but I felt good about it, knowing we had worked hard.

The grunts had it easy compared to Evans. They were in the field for only two weeks and then in the rear for seven days. We were serving in a relatively friendly area; there were very few, if any, NVA regulars. The VC were the problem, and then only at night. Because of proximity of the Air Force and its many gunships, no major battles were expected. There was no good bush country for the grunts, but compared to Evans, it was a piece of cake.

To add to S-4's troubles, Colonel Steverson didn't feel that the outer base camps were very secure. Therefore, he thought the 101st should show those other units how to build one.

I thought he saw that the men were going to be bored if they weren't kept busy, so if we built a new firebase, all would be well. The problem of furnishing the materials, of course, fell on my shoulders. My country living experience helped tremendously at that point. We had no engineers assigned to S-4, so we had to figure out the required material ourselves. Since I was only authorized about one tenth of what was needed, I promised the colonel nothing, and again was told to do my best.

Wooldridge and I had been to every proper channel at this point, and no amount of paper work was going to get us seventeen semi-trailer loads of lumber. And the one request I just knew was impossible was chain-link fence. But, like Dad had always said, "Bitchin' and worryin' won't get anything done." So I cornered about four of the S-4 people and explained our situation.

They had the look on their faces that told me not only was the colonel crazy, but that old Don wasn't too bright for even thinking about trying to deliver. But I just told Sergeant Wade that he was going to be in charge because Tom Wooldridge and I would be busy scrounging for several days.

As soon as our little meeting broke up, an Air Force medic truck pulled in, and a short, wiry career sergeant came in to grace the doorstep of my humble S-4 office. We visited for about two hours, and I learned more from him in a short time about Cam Ranh Bay than I ever expected to know. Finally, he figured he could trust me and told me why he had come by. It seemed that he had a need for something that only a few grunts could boast—enemy rifles and souvenirs of the NVA and VC.

I knew that a real fish was on my line, so I figured to make the bait more tantalizing by showing him the connex full of captured weapons. When I opened up the connex, I knew that he was hooked. At that time, we had three connexes full of stuff with at least 250 AK-47s, SKSs (Russian semiautomatic rifles), and a few homemade guns. There were crossbows, knives, clothing, compasses—you name it, and we had either found or captured it in the past. Each item had been tagged for the unit that had obtained it.

At first he said that all he wanted was one AK-47 and one SKS rifle. I gave him the bloody war story behind each rifle and captured item. Now I don't care much for liars, but in that case I may have spiced up my story a little. I picked up an AK-47 with my old platoon's name tag on it and told him how we had captured an NVA colonel and fifteen men all carrying the new Russian AK-47s. My fish was getting bigger with every word.

I think what finally hooked the sergeant was when I explained how we got some of the SKSs. I told him how we'd ambushed a small group of VC one night and that they had all been young women each carrying rice and SKSs with several rounds of ammunition.

His eyes got about the size of silver dollars, and I knew that anything he owned was mine for the asking. I closed up the connexes before my stories got too unbelievable and I lost him, or at least before Wooldridge burst out laughing.

A couple of beers later, he popped the right question as to how he could own a couple of those rifles. I gave him the old military excuse about how much trouble I could get into if I gave them to anyone other than those they'd been tagged for. He started offering goods that I wasn't sure he could deliver. He named medical supplies, sheets, pillows, and pillow cases.

"What in the hell would grunts do with sheets and pillow cases?" I asked. I knew, however, that the colonel and I would sleep much better between white sheets.

The sergeant then asked what we could use, so I thought I

would see how well I had him hooked. I suggested a case of steaks every week while we were there, and good bourbon whiskey, which we never had. He said it would be tough, but he would be back the next day with everything he could find; however, he said he might need a few more rifles.

My answer was that I would radio some of the men for permission to give up their hard-earned booty. I assured him that I could get at least two weapons, seeing as how my old platoon had been the one that had captured the colonel and the women. Wooldridge just about spat up his beer, and I was glad he was where the sergeant couldn't see him. The sergeant left, promising me anything he could find would be there at about 1800 hours the next day.

14

The next day, Tom and I drove all over the Air Force and Navy compounds trying to get the material for the colonel's firebase. We came up with the fact that everything we needed was on the boat docks, but it lacked the paper work. It would soon be heading for Air Force officer clubs and far-off destinations.

We ate our evening chow and were feeling pretty low when in pulled two covered trucks from the Air Force. They were one-and-a-half-ton medical trucks, and the men inside, both sergeants, had smiles about a mile long. I knew some luck was on my side.

We went into my little office and closed the door. Tom couldn't stand the suspense and came in with us. The sergeant introduced his buddy and started reciting all the items on the trucks that they would trade for two AK-47s and one SKS, plus a crossbow with at least five arrows.

The other sergeant was a meat inspector for the Air Force. He rode around in the meat trucks delivering all the staples to Air Force mess halls. He assured me that every Thursday he would come by and kick off a case of condemned steaks and twenty-five gallons of peaches or something similar. The condemned signs would be his cover in case he was questioned.

We went out to the trucks to look at all the goods.

"Sergeant," I said, "I think we might be able to deal if I can get a carton of Marlboros each week. If you can assure me of the steaks and peaches, as well as the Marlboros, I'll tell you what I'll do. We'll unload this tonight and I'll give you one AK and one SKS. Next week, if you deliver, I'll give you dirty sheets for clean ones in exchange for another AK or whatever you need. Each week you deliver, I'll deliver."

We shook hands and started unloading. I was really pleased with the deal, and I got a bigger shock when they unloaded the steaks. I knew that back home a case of anything was twelve, twenty-four, or thirty-six, but in Nam, a case of steaks was 148 prime steaks. They also brought out twenty cases of all types of whiskey.

I felt so bad about the deal that I threw in an extra SKS to seal our friendship. As they were leaving, the sergeant told me to forget his name at all cost, and to this day I won't mention his name or unit. But the Air Force had a good man who knew that the infantry needed steak and whiskey.

Later, after swearing the mess sergeant to secrecy, we laid out a plan to feed every trooper on stand-down a steak. And once a week, too.

That would leave about forty-eight steaks. The colonel was to get a steak sandwich before retiring each night, and S-4 and the mess hall would share the rest among themselves and the other officers. In fact, we fried one on the spot, and it sure tasted good.

We also agreed to make an outdoor grill. When the troops rotated in, they would have cold beer and a steak, hot off the grill. We would seal the colonel's mouth with a case of whiskey.

About 9 P.M., I told the colonel I had a few things for him if he would allow us to redecorate his hootch. He was busy playing bridge and gave us permission to clean up or do whatever was needed.

Tom and I brought over some clean sheets and placed a little meal ticket by his table. It was good for one bedtime steak sandwich each night before retiring, plus an unlimited supply of whiskey for his guests.

We had four cases of Canadian Club which was so rare I couldn't believe our good fortune. We placed one whole case of CC under the colonel's bed and left a paper arrow on the floor pointing toward the cache. In one corner, we stacked enough clean sheets to last for ninety days, and we left a sign saying, "Compliments of S-4 3/187th."

I felt really good inside. I left for the S-4 office where Tom and I had made our plans for the next day. My idea was to take our dirtiest jeep and put on my worst looking bush clothes and old worn jungle boots. Tom was to dress the same and to back up anything I'd say, especially if it was stretching the truth a little.

The next morning at 5:30, the colonel wanted to see me, so I headed to his office dressed in the worst looking jungle outfit I had. He looked me over from head to toe and then started chewing my ass like I didn't think possible. His main thrust was that under no condition would he accept favors when the men didn't have the same entitlements. He also told me that the doctor had reported finding a full list of supplies that were marked for the Air Force. On top of it all, he said that the head of S-4 could at least dress properly in clean clothes and boots.

I wasn't sure where to start, so I just spilled the beans and started telling him everything. About halfway through he just grinned and said, "Say no more."

I assured him that my first concern was always for the grunts in the field and that I didn't consider the Air Force and Navy enemies, but sources of supply.

"This poor farm boy is about to embark on a mercy mission for the Army to supply his colonel with wire and lumber for his base camp," I said.

"Where's it coming from?" he asked.

I started to divulge my plan, but again, halfway through, he held up his hand.

"Say no more," he said. "I'll hang. The less I know, the better."

I told him that if my plan worked, I would need to get the stuff out of there the same day it came in. Colonel Steverson told me he would see to it that it was disposed of immediately.

"Colonel," I said before I left, "if some unhappy Air Force colonel or general calls, you might act a little shocked and even a little mad at being accused of skullduggery."

"If I don't know about it, I can't be responsible, so have at it as long as it's honest, Lieutenant Stephen. You build me a firebase, and I'll handle any unhappy people."

He was smiling with every word he spoke.

"By the way," I told him. "There is a belly dancer at the Air Force officers' club tonight, but don't expect their whiskey selection to be the best. It seems someone ripped off twenty cases of whiskey, so they'll be a little short until next week's shipment comes in."

"You've got twenty cases?" he started in disbelief. "Never mind, I don't want to know any more. Just see to it that the troops are taken care of. Now get out before I have a migraine headache."

Tom and I loaded up four cases of whiskey, and to hide them, we placed C-rations all around, so it looked like we were hauling a whole jeep of Cs.

Our first step was to get all we could through the proper channels. One semi-trailer load of lumber was granted, as well as three loads of concertina wire, but I was sure it had been done only because I'd bugged them to death. I told Tom that the only thing left was begging or rerouting materials.

The next place we stopped was the junk yard. Everything that the Air Force, Army, or Navy decided was junk ended up there. We had to bribe an NCO to get through the gate. He eyebrowed our C-rations and told us two cases would allow us entry.

I'd never seen anything like it in my life. Everything a person could imagine was there, and by the thousands.

We found about ten connexes full of chain saws. Most of them looked good, but didn't run for one reason or another. The only things we took were ponchos and poncho liners, which only had a few holes the size of a nickel. Most of them were in better shape than those the grunts were using in the field, but we could never get enough though normal channels.

We got back to the guard station and found a lieutenant there along with the sergeant. The sarge looked a little sheepish, and I soon found out why.

The lieutenant jumped right astride of me and told me no one was allowed in or out of there unless they had paper work or were Vietnamese. I could tell I had a lifer on my hands—one who went by the books. And I was in ragged clothes and a dirty jeep.

I tried sensible tactics on the lieutenant, but he just kept getting madder and madder. I then tried a different approach and asked where all the stuff was going. His reply was sharp and quick. Anything the Vietnamese didn't want was going to be burned and buried.

I nearly croaked. And then I got hot. In fifty words or less, I told him the facts of life about being a grunt and that all the stuff could be used for a better cause than giving it to the Vietnamese or burning it.

The lieutenant was going to call the MP and have me escorted out of the area. I asked to see his commanding officer and was gladly taken up on the offer. I figured I had made a big mistake, as eager as he was, but I was like an old snapping turtle. Once I was mad, I bit into the problem, even if somebody chopped my head off; but if they did, they'd know I'd been there. I figured a few tracks in the sands of life were better than no tracks at all.

I expected a captain, but not a major. I had nothing personal against majors, but they seemed to have a lot against life. Just about any officer would make major, unless he was a real dud in life, but only a small percentage of majors ever made lieutenant colonel, and even fewer made full-bird colonel. If a major hung around long enough, he eventually made light colonel. I always figured that was the reason majors were so hard to live with.

This guy was sloppy and looked like he had been passed over for colonel at least a half dozen times. The lieutenant told him the story, and the only good thing about it was that the jeep ride to the major's hootch had cooled him off a little, so I didn't argue. I was used to people sticking together, no matter what the situation was. One thing about a grunt was that he fought for his fellow grunt, even if his comrade was wrong. I figured I'd take a good tongue-lashing and head for clearer waters.

The old major excused the lieutenant and told him not to let anyone else go rummaging through his rat yard. He told me to be seated and to smoke if I wanted. I lit up a Marlboro and thought if I had a blindfold, I'd be ready to be shot.

"Now, no bullshit, no lying, just tell me the truth," he began. "How did you get past the guard tower?"

"Two cases of Cs," I answered. I hated to get the sergeant in trouble, but my unit came first.

"Times have changed when Cs can bribe one of my men," the major said.

"I was prepared to offer more," I told him, seeing an opening.

"Such as?"

"Whatever it takes to supply my outfit."

"Do you have any field time?" he asked.

"Six-and-a-half months in the bush on Lom San 719. I'm new to the S-4 job ... I hope the sergeant doesn't get into too much trouble. He seemed to understand the facts of life, but the lifer lieutenant didn't." I wanted to kick myself for saying lifer, but it was too late

"I don't like a lot of young lifers either," the major replied. "But I'm from the old school, and I hope you don't consider me a lifer in the bad sense of the word."

"I'll reserve my decision until I leave your office," I said coolly.

"Explain." He got out a pack of Kents. I offered him a Marlboro which he took gratefully, so I offered him a whole pack of my precious Marls.

He took them and I explained that our supply of basic necessities for the men in the field had always been short and that he had plenty of surplus, such as the poncho liners hidden in my jeep. He cautioned me about lying, and I assured him that I wasn't.

"Every soldier is issued one of each," he said. "Where are they all being lost?"

"Body bags and the jungle," I said.

"What do you need?"

"Anything I can get my hands on that's of use to an infantry battalion," I replied. "Give me twelve hours of rummaging though your junk with one deuce-and-a-half and six men, and you'll never see me again."

"It'll have to be on a Wednesday. The IG (Inspector General) constantly watches over the division. He hasn't had trouble with the Americans, but the civilian gooks are constantly sneaking in. If you get caught, I'll be a major for a while longer. I know the full-bird personally, but he's a stickler for detail. But if I can get him drunk Tuesday night, he probably won't feel up to an inspection on Wednesday."

I offered some Canadian Club for the cause, and his eyes couldn't have lit up more if I'd paraded ten naked women and given him his choice. He asked if Jack Daniel's would be around anywhere, and that time my eyes were the ones that lit up because I had both brands in the jeep.

"Come with me to the jeep," I beckoned.

Tom started unloading the jeep for the third time. I reached in and brought out a bottle of JD light and JD dark and one Canadian Club.

"What would it take for more?" he asked, giving me a funny look.

"I'll give you two cases for some information."

"Shoot."

"Who hauls all this junk here?" I asked.

"The main motor pool for all of Cam Ranh Bay. They haul it in everything from one-on trucks to semis to S-and-P trailers."

"If you had a bunch of stuff to move without paper work, how would you do it?" I asked.

"With those C-rations, a little beer, and that whiskey, those truck drivers will do anything," he said, smiling.

I thanked him and handed him three cases of whiskey. He was like a country boy in a candy store. I told him that some Air Force officer was going to be dry for a week because the major'd be drinking Air Force hootch. He just about fell down laughing.

"We have to go to the Air Force officers' club to get a good mixed drink, and those guys are always laughing about the Army supply line."

"Well, Major," I said. "You have the upper hand for one week because they are short twenty cases of the best, and they will be five cases short per week for the next ten weeks."

Just as we were leaving, I said, "You're the best lifer I've ever met. We'll see you Wednesday."

He got really serious and said, "Take care of the sergeant at the guardhouse, and he'll take care of you."

We left and started driving around looking for different things we could use. We drove onto the Air Force base, and to get by the AP (air patrol), we had to lie and say we were visiting wounded in the hospital. Finally, after a bit of driving, I noticed several oxygen and acetylene tanks stored inside a chain-link fence.

We stopped, and I was wishing for a cutting torch head and a way of relieving the Air Force of a few tanks when an Air Force sergeant came up and asked what we were doing. I told him what we needed.

"No way," he said. "The Air Force keeps strict records of every little item, and anyone caught stealing is in big trouble."

"I'm not going to steal anything," I answered. "But I'll trade some damaged equipment for good stuff."

"No way," he said again.

I finally explained in detail how he could accomplish all the paper work of exchanging junk for the real thing. He'd have a few extra things at the end of his tour of duty and the taxpayers back home could see that their dollars were being spent on American soldiers instead of Vietnamese.

So two homemade Chinese knives and a case of whiskey later, the deal was settled.

Tom and I headed back for the Third, 187th, feeling pretty good about our day's work. We were looking forward to a nice mixed drink with real ice, and a big, juicy steak. I slept well that night, feeling pretty proud of myself. I could hardly wait for the next few days to see if I could pull it off

The next morning, Sergeant Wade told me that the only chain-link fence in Vietnam was in the Saigon area, and there was no way we could get any of it up north without someone of high rank asking for it.

"Your lieutenant bars just aren't big enough," the sergeant said.

A thought crossed my mind, and I was sure it wouldn't work, but the best way for a person to get on his feet is to get off his ass, so I called the engineer battalion in Saigon that had a whole shipload of chain-link fence.

We had two captains in our battalion whose fathers were generals. I had no idea whether they were active or retired, but it was worth a shot.

"This is Captain Zais," I spoke when a captain answered my call. "I'm still looking for my shipment of chain-link fence to Cam Ranh Bay."

"No chain-link fence is available, except in the Saigon area, and there is no paper work of any orders from up north," was his answer.

"Captain, I'll tell you what I'm going to do," I said. "I need enough chain-link fence to cover a mile, and I'll give you thirty minutes to check out and see if the names General Berry and General Zais mean anything at all down south. If they don't, then I won't bother you anymore directly, but I will have the generals do my talking for me. If I need paper work, I will sign for the material when it gets here, or else I'll send a few trucks after."

I called back exactly thirty minutes later. They were loading General Berry's chain-link fence to be sent out the next morning by truck. It seemed they had several things on the dock at Cam Ranh Bay to pick up, anyway, and it would be no trouble to deliver it, but it would be at least three days in getting there. I apologized for my abruptness over the phone, explaining how our paper work kept getting lost somehow.

"We have to be real careful these days because so many people are stealing everything," the captain told me.

I agreed wholeheartedly that it was a shame we couldn't trust anyone anymore.

After I hung up the phone, I stood up, and my knees were shaking, and I felt nauseated, so I sat back down.

"Lieutenant, if they don't catch you, then you ought to write a book someday," Wooldridge said.

I told him if they caught me, I would have plenty of time

to write from my jail cell. I thought about what I'd done, and deep down inside, I didn't feel like I was doing anything immoral. All I was doing was taking the mismanagement of citizens' tax dollars and placing the priority back where it belonged—in the U.S. Army infantry. My method may have been questionable, but my motive was sincere and proper. The grunt was on the low end of the totem pole in everything, yet the grunt was the backbone of the U.S. military and deserved better treatment. I rationalized that as long as I didn't have to pay out of my own pocket, I would go home to that rich Illinois soil no worse for the wear.

I went over to the colonel's office and told him everything would be ready within the week, or not at all.

"Just do it, because time is running out," the colonel said. "I figured it'll take thirty days to finish the firebase. The men are digging foxholes now and will be ready for the lumber."

"Your chain-link, compliments of General Berry, is on its way," I said. "And I'll have heavy metal for the top of the bunkers."

"How are we going to get a group of engineers to cut the metal and place it?" Colonel Steverson asked.

"We'll have to do it ourselves," I answered. "But we have ten cutting torches and enough gas and oxygen to build one firebase only. If none of the troops know how to use them, I can teach a few men to cut flat metal in minutes."

The colonel was staring at me, and I thought it best to leave before he learned too much of the details. Tom and I headed for the main motor pool to see what we could do. He had already packed the jeep with a few souvenirs and some whiskey, hidden under all the C-rations.

The main motor pool was a sight to behold. It must have been a mile square and chock full of every jeep, truck, and car imaginable. I didn't know who to see, so we drove around and talked to a few GIs who were hanging around, and it didn't feel right until we came upon a card game in the back of a deuce-

and-a-half. I broke out a bottle of whiskey and put it in my fatigue shirt. I walked up to the truck and one guy saw me.

"Ah, shit!" he said. "Don't you officers have anything better to do than bother the enlisted men?"

"Not if you need information as badly as I do," I replied. "And I need some who can talk freely and not get another man in trouble."

They offered me a beer and invited me in, so I crawled in the back and saw they were playing poker.

"Don't let me interrupt." I pulled out a twenty dollar MPC (Military Payment Certificates) bill and set it on the table which was a small crate or ammo box. Then I set the whiskey down. One private eyeballed the whiskey, so I opened the bottle and passed it to the left.

"Deal the cards," I said. When I'd first crawled into the truck there had been no money showing, but it started appearing fast, and there was quite a lot of it.

"I'd sell my soul for some Jack Daniel's sipping whiskey," one young soldier from Oklahoma said.

"I prefer Canadian Club," I answered. "But if your soul is for sale, I can furnish the Jack Daniel's for one day's worth of your soul."

They never even dealt the cards but wanted to know what I needed. So I told them I needed twenty S-and-P trailer trucks for one day, and that I'd furnish a quart of whiskey and two cases of beer per driver, and, for this group of five, a case of whiskey and whatever it took to get them to find the trucks and drivers.

"And you gotta forget where you deliver the lumber," I added.

At first they looked dumbfounded, and then they smiled, and one asked if any drugs were involved.

"Boys, I want to do business with you, but I don't deal in anything like that, including Mary Jane. What you do with your booze is your problem, but all I want is what the grunts in the

field have coming to them. Everything I want will be used by
GIs for their protection, and I'm pissed at the Air Force and
Navy because they have it all, and I just want a little. What I'm
proposing to do is reroute the lumber destined to build an Air
Force officers' club, and ship it out to my battalion to build a
firebase to protect lives. If you're not interested, just say so
and I'll leave."

The oldest looking soldier might have been twenty-one.
They looked at each other for a minute, and the grizzly looking
twenty-one-year-old asked, "How do we get by with it, and not
end up in the stockade?"

I told them my neck was on the line at the shipyard, but
once we left there, all they had to do was deliver and keep their
mouths shut about where they delivered it to. Since so many
trucks were involved, nobody would be after the drivers for
doing what they were told to do.

I had checked it out earlier. These guys were always traveling Route 1, delivering up and down, and they were gone for
two or three days sometimes.

"In three days," I said, "over one hundred S-and-Ps will
be loaded for delivery. All you have to do is be there first, so
you can load and deliver and then get back in line for your
proper load. If you can get loaded first, you'll be back sitting in
line in two hours."

They were in unanimous agreement. They would try it, if
for no other reason than to put one over on the Air Force officers. The fact that they would only be a few hours late was enough
to convince them. The plan made sense to them. They shook
hands, and I gave them each a case of whiskey.

"When should you be in line?" I asked them.

"The Navy dock workers don't go to work until seven.
And it's unusual to have trucks waiting in line at 0500. If we
check out our trucks at 3:30 A.M., we can be in line at 4 A.M."

"I'll be there at 4 A.M. with the whiskey and beer, and
maybe a few extra surprises," I told them. "If you're sure you

can have twenty trucks in line and ready to go, and you can be trusted, then we'll score a major victory over the Air Force and Navy."

Tom and I left. We would check the night before to be sure everything was set.

On the way back, I told him that the stage was set, and if it all worked out, it would be a miracle. But deep inside, I felt the need to carry it out to the end for the glory of the 101st Air Mobile.

We returned to the battalion area, and the colonel wanted to see me. Captain Bobadillo of Bravo Company was there. Colonel Steverson told me the captain was upset about the re-supply for his men.

"Everything I have is available," I said. "But if it isn't in the compound, I can't send it out. Besides, some of the stuff I send out isn't even authorized. And Bravo is the worst for re-turning things, and when they do return items, they are either broken or totally useless."

The captain really chewed my ass, and the colonel let him do it. My dad used to tell me that when a man was mad, there was no reasoning with him, and the best thing to do was keep quiet until the water cooled. So I just took the ass-chewing.

Captain Bobadillo left.

"Well, I hope you understand that the men in the field come first," said the colonel.

"Colonel, I'm so mad right now that I only have one thing to say. I took this job to do nothing but make it better for my friends in the bush, and at anytime you don't like what I'm doing, you can send me back to the bush."

I started to leave and then turned, "All your damned mate-rial will be at the firebase site in three days. I have only one request."

"Name it."

"The trucks have to be unloaded as fast as possible. The men can stack it neatly later, but it is imperative to get the trucks out right away or the Air Force might be a little upset."

"I don't want to know anything," the colonel agreed as I left, "but I'll pass the word."

I don't think I've ever been so mad in my life. Now I've been pretty mad before, but I had tears in my eyes this time. I hated Bobadillo and the whole mess I was in. I told Tom that I was going over to the Air Force officers' club to get so drunk that I would have to crawl home, and nobody was to try to stop me.

I changed my clothes and drove over to the club. I started drinking doubles, and after about an hour of sitting alone, Lieutenant Mullens and Lieutenant Laporo from Bravo Company came in. They have both been classmates of Mike Dalton and had come in-country about two weeks after I had. They joined me and asked what was happening.

"I'm getting drunk. If you want to join, you're welcome. But I'm telling you that the reason is your damned lifer, Captain Bobadillo."

They assured me he was the best captain in the field.

"Bullshit!" I exclaimed. "He's the biggest asshole in the bush. He's always chewing my ass over the radio, and now he's done it in front of the colonel." I looked up at them. "I've just got one question for you guys. Since I've taken over S-4, has your resupply been better or worse? And I want an honest answer."

Their reply was what I expected. Things were about the same, with some improvement, such as ice and hot meals.

"Next week, if everything works out, you won't be short anything. But I'm not going to take any more ass-chewings like I did today. And I don't care if he is a captain."

They kept telling me that Bobadillo wasn't that kind of guy, but I wouldn't listen. We talked about the bush for a while, and Lieutenant Mullens put a big wad of chew in his mouth, then lit a cigar. I never did see him spit all evening, and he drank beer on top of it all.

When I get mad, my adrenaline or whatever, allows me to

go for hours feeling no pain. I was fully alert and sober as a judge at 9:05 P.M. when Captain Bobadillo came in. He sat down at our table, laughing and joking, and I just sat there staring at him

"Lieutenant," the captain said, "you should be back at headquarters doing your job for grunts instead of being here partying."

I flew out of my chair, and I'm not sure what I said to him, but after I said it I walked out to the jeep. I lay my head on the steering wheel and cried, not like a baby, but with tears of hatred. Everything was a blur. I contemplated beating the captain to a pulp, and I was just ready to go inside when Moon Mullens came out.

"Go tell your captain I've had it, and there are two ways he can handle it. One is to come out here and be whipped like a dog. If he doesn't, and he thinks his resupply is fucked up now, just wait till he sees what he gets later. Go tell him, Mullens, because if he isn't man enough to come out here within ten minutes, I'm leaving. And I'll consider Bravo Company's commander a big cherry pussy."

Moon (Mullens) tried to reason with me, but I would have none of it. About five minutes later, Captain Bobadillo came out, and this time he spoke very carefully. He first apologized for his behavior, and I was shocked. He explained that his only motive was to get everything he could for his troops. The captain I had replaced hadn't given a shit about anything, and he had had to jack him up every three days just to get normal resupply.

"Well, I'm here to tell you first of all that I ain't no captain. I served my time in the bush. I ain't no lifer, and if I say I don't have something, then I don't have it, and you can jack me all you want, but you ain't gonna get it."

"I realize that now," he said. "There won't be any more trouble."

The anger left me with each word he spoke. I could see

how I would have done the same thing had I been a captain in the field.

"Are you going to hold a grudge against Bravo Company?"

"Captain, I couldn't short anyone in the field because I've been there, and that's probably where I belong. What I said was in the heat of anger, and I apologize for saying it."

"Call me Bob," he held out his hand. "And let's bury the hatchet."

I took his hand and offered to buy him a drink in my hootch, and he jumped in the jeep. Needless to say, he was my kind of man, and we became friends that night. Had we had the chance to be together, I think he could have replaced Mike Dalton as that close, trusted friend.

15

The next day marked forty-five days at Cam Ranh Bay. I had a good group of REMFs, and everything was going well. Bob took me over to the colonel's office and got me off the hook there, so I felt pretty good.

It was Wednesday and time to go after all the stuff at the junk yard. Everything went well, and we got just about all we needed. We had two deuce-and-a-half trucks full of ponchos, poncho liners, canteens, compasses, and about two hundred chain saws.

When we returned to headquarters, we found several Red Cross girls causing quite a stir. They were passing out short-timer calendars and SP packs, which were supply packs that contained toilet articles and candy. Short-timer calendars came in all shapes and sizes as well as different numbers of days.

Every grunt wanted one, but it wasn't military for officers and high-ranking sergeants to have one; however, I was getting short myself, so I took a short-timer calendar and hung it over my desk.

The rumors of going home were flying around everywhere. The only rumor I cared about was the one about lieutenants getting out as much as two months early. Now that was something to look forward to. If it was true, I was down to sixty days left in-country, and that beat 120 all to hell.

There were a lot of jokes about being short, such as, "I'm so short, I have to have a ladder to get on the shitter." A pure short-timer was less than thirty days and counting. And if you wanted to meet a tight asshole, seven days and counting was really tight.

My old platoon had received several replacements from other battalions, so I felt better about deserting them. I saw them every time they came in on stand-down. I felt if I could just pull off my escapade at the boat yard, I would go home happy—as happy as could be expected considering the circumstances.

I marked my short-timer calendar and my Greenwell Funeral Home calendar, one at sixty days, and one at 120 days. If the lumber plan worked out, I could begin to relax in just forty-eight hours. The only difference between the amount of sleep in the rear and in the bush was the safety factor, plus the fact that no one woke me up for guard duty.

The next day was peaceful, and all went well, so Tom and I rested up for the following day, knowing it was going to be long and nerve-racking. From the colonel on down, I knew they did not realize how much lumber would be on seventeen semi-trucks, and how much barbed wire would be on three semis. But I hoped they would find out.

I had the proper paper work for one semi-trailer load of lumber and for three loads of barbed wire. But somehow the paper work ended up at seventeen loads of lumber instead of one. I just figured the good Lord agreed with me that the Army grunt needed it more than the Air Force.

Tom and I loaded a one-ton truck full of beer, whiskey, extra C-rations, a few war souvenirs, pillows, and pillow cases. I drove the truck, and we headed for the shipyard to meet the drivers. I figured deep down inside me that the trucks would never show up. But all I could do was wait and see.

At four o'clock no one had shown up, and I felt defeated. Then, at 4:30 A.M., there they were. Not twenty trucks, but twenty-four semi-trailers, nose to tail, just like elephants.

The twenty-one-year-old was first in line. I jumped on his door and shook his hand.

"You had me worried!" I yelled above the crank of diesel.

"Well, the lieutenant and dispatcher couldn't believe that we wanted to get going so early," he said, "and we had to talk hard to get away."

"Is it all that unusual to cause a big stir?"

"It isn't all that unusual for most drivers," he said, grinning, "but for this bunch ... it's unheard of!"

"I asked for only twenty trucks. How come twenty-four?"

He smiled again.

"There was no way I could keep it from happening. Several more wanted to come, so we had to agree to share or you would have had the whole hundred here."

"Man, I'll be lucky to get by with forged papers for twenty, let alone twenty-four," I exclaimed.

He assured me they had paper work for up north and that they were going to play follow the leader and accidentally dump their loads with the rest.

"Well, we've come this far," I said. "Why not all the way? If you'll help distribute the goods, I'll send Tom back for four extra helpings of booty."

"I don't want to be an asshole," the driver said, "but five of us worked pretty hard to help you, and we thought just maybe we ought to get a little extra."

I was already ahead of him.

"No problem, but if my name ever gets out, I will send my whole unit to kick somebody's ass."

"You probably would," he grinned again, "but not to worry. These men are used to fucking up, but they are experts at covering up as well."

I sent Tom back for extra booze, and as I drove the ton truck along, they unloaded two cases of beer and one bottle of whiskey per truck. I offered them the C-rations and bedding material, and they accepted.

By five o'clock, more trucks were starting to arrive, and we didn't look quite so suspicious. Tom showed up, and we unloaded the last four drivers' hooch, then drove to the front of the line. From the front seat of the truck, I handed the driver an extra case of whiskey, a few North Vietnamese knives, and then dug out two SKS rifles under wrap so nobody would see them.

They were ecstatic. They swore they would die before they gave me away.

We all opened up some C-rations for breakfast, and several played cards in the dark, flicking their BICs occasionally to see what they had.

At about 6:30 A.M., I tied my leech straps on and got my M-16. I had no need for these since leaving the bush, but I just couldn't turn in old friends until it was time to go home.

At about 6:50 A.M., the Navy changed its guard for the day. The man in the cage whom I had tried to bribe a couple of weeks earlier was back on duty. Now I don't know Navy rank from apple butter, but he was enlisted and had all kinds of hash marks on his sleeve. We hadn't liked each other too well on our first few meetings, and I didn't expect to get along now. But the fire fight's not over till the dead are counted, so I headed toward him. He saluted me.

"I hope you have the paper work this time," he said.

"Mister, I've fought hard to get this paper work. All this red tape is a bunch of bullshit. I've heard how you guys redirect supplies and blackmarket all the material, and now that

I've spent days of bullshit, I'm going to stand here and guard every damned board and every damned nail. Everything I get better be number-one pine lumber or I'll reject it."

Now the secret to getting a man's goat and convincing him that you're sincere is in knowing when to quit. I knew that patriotism was his weak point because he was a lifer, so I finished by saying, "The Army doesn't have one enlisted club or officers' club, and I found out a lot of your lumber is for Air Force and Navy clubs and hootches, so if you begrudge the infantry a few loads of lumber to protect a few lives, then I'll spend the rest of my tour of duty digging into every little item and writing my congressman."

He was red up to his ears by then, so I shut up.

"Lieutenant, I pride myself in the fact that no one has stolen even the first board while I've been on duty. I realize there is a lot of injustice in our supply, but I'm just doing my job."

"I'm sorry," I said. "But if you knew the bullshit I had to go through to get this much when I need ten times as much, you would be upset, too. I've tried bribery to the fullest extent, and all I got for my trouble is twenty measly truckloads, and if I hadn't bugged those people so much I wouldn't have gotten this much. I personally escorted these drivers over here, and I hope I don't lose any of them."

"No problem," he said. "I understand, but I have had experts try to rip me off."

They had offered him everything from money to women. He wished that just once there would be a friendly gesture with no string attached.

"I'm sorry," I said again. "If you just get my trucks loaded, I won't bother you anymore."

I stuck out my hand and we shook. He told me to pull my trucks in. He had moe than one hundred trucks to load that day, but mine were first in line.

"When you're done, you'll have to sign for everything, and that'll be the end of it," he said.

He had mentioned that he was the only one who hadn't been ripped off, so I asked him what had happened to the other guys who had been.

"So far, it's been of such small magnitude that they were able to reshuffle paper," he answered. "There are thousands of items going every direction, so it really isn't that hard to cover up as much as fifty truckloads if necessary. But I hope it never happens to me because in ninety days I'm retiring from the Navy."

By 9 A.M., all the trucks were loaded and ready. Tom and the first driver came up to me. I grabbed the clipboard and Tom talked to the Navy man while I scraped the seven off of seventeen and signed my name. The crucial time had arrived. If he noticed the change, all hell would break loose. If he didn't, we were home free.

I handed him the clipboard. He looked at it, then stepped back into his cage since other drivers were waiting with paper work. I walked over to the jeep and grabbed a case of C-rations and a homemade VC knife and brought them over to the cage.

"It isn't very much," I said, "but I'm sorry for the way I talked. If I can get some more paper work, I'll be back."

"Anytime," he told me.

Other trucks were waiting behind ours, so I led the way and Tom followed the twenty-fourth truck. When we got to the firebase ten miles away, the colonel was there. We pulled the trucks around in a huge circle, and I jumped on the first truck and started unchaining and then just kicking the lumber off as quickly as possible. Within twenty minutes they were ready to leave. I shook hands with the five drivers and wished them luck on their return. I supposed all went well because I never heard from them again.

Twenty-one loads of lumber and three loads of barbed wire looked like one hell of a mess, but it was ours, and given about a week, it would be cut up, and a lot of it buried for bunkers.

The colonel called me over and took me inside.

"Couldn't we have unloaded it a little neater?" he asked.

"Colonel, those drivers had to get back in line by 11:30 to get their real load."

He just shook his head.

"I'd give you a medal," he smiled, "but I don't think it would be okayed without a few questions."

"I don't need medals," I answered. "Just appreciation for taking care of the troops."

Tom and I spent the rest of the day building sawhorses and cutting lumber. During the next few days, I would have given anything for my dad and his shop. Before I was drafted, I had helped my uncle, Bob Stephen, build pole buildings for farmers. That experience came in handy at Cam Ranh Bay since we were building an authorized firebase with unauthorized material. We didn't have engineers and carpenters, except a few like myself, so we made do.

I left a week later because Second Platoon was coming in for stand-down, and I wanted to see how the guys were doing. When I returned to headquarters, the colonel was jubilant. He had received only one phone call. It had informed him that someone had stolen some lumber and to be on the lookout for a short, freckle-faced lieutenant from some unknown Army unit.

"I've done nothing wrong on paper," I protested. "I just signed my name for one S-and-P trailer of lumber and three loads of concertina wire."

"Don't worry about it," he laughed. "It was the Air Force who called. Not the proper channels. They seem to have lost a bunch of whiskey and lumber, and they are a little upset."

"I never stole anything in the line of whiskey. Each week I find some cases in my supply room, and they don't have anyone's name on them. ... If they're short, you might offer them a little to get them by for a while. As for the lumber, as long as S-4 command or a Navy petty officer doesn't call me by name, then I knew nothing. And even if they do, my name is signed on the proper paper work."

"I did have one odd phone call from the Saigon area wanting to speak to Captain Zais about some chain-link fence," the colonel mused. "But I handled it okay."

"I have a tape of my conversation with Saigon," I explained. "And I did drop a few big names. But if they had listened to what I said, they would never have sent us anything."

"From now on, Lieutenant, I'll be careful about what I ask from S-4," he chuckled.

I'd enjoyed the whole adventure immensely, but I wasn't sure how much more I could stand. That night, my nerves caught up with me and I slept for twelve straight hours, and nobody woke me up.

16

By the end of August, the firebase was built and everyone had settled into a routine. The colonel hadn't come up with any major plans since we would be going north in a few days. I had ample time to drive around and check out Cam Ranh Bay.

The Air Force had closed down its enlisted men's club, or at least they'd put it off limits to Army grunts. The only way to get on the Air Force base was to go to the hospital to visit wounded or sick.

But the Navy club in Cam Ranh Bay was a different story. I was sure that money was changing hands somewhere or else the grunts simply spent enough money in there to keep everyone happy. When my old platoon came in, I would spend a lot of time at the club with the men.

It was an enormous club and could seat several hundred people. I'm not sure whether they served hard liquor, although beer alone was enough to swirl the brain. But they did have Vietnamese gals waiting on the tables, plus live entertainment every night.

The problem stemmed from the fact that the grunts had a little money, and it meant absolutely nothing to them. The Navy men, on the other hand, had been stationed there the whole time and had all the girls sewn up at a cheap price.

Both the Navy and Air Force were paying about two dollars for a girl, but when the grunts came to town they would spend whatever it took and didn't hassle too much on price. I think that was the prime reason behind the Navy men getting upset so easily. Add that to the fact that a grunt demanded respect for his position and you had trouble.

"Lord help the man who treads on a grunt's toes" seemed to fit the situation. Some would call it *esprit de corps*. It really boiled down to protection of our own, whether we even liked them. If a man's life depended on his fellow grunt, then that grunt could do no wrong.

Some of the men hadn't seen a woman in six months, and that fact, combined with money in the pocket and booze on the brain, caused some Navy men a few problems. The 101st grunt didn't care who the women belonged to; they were all going to be had for the taking. Now I'm not saying the Screaming Eagles kicked ass and won every fight. In fact, the Navy probably won its share of the battles. But a Screaming Eagle was always around, and he kept coming back for more.

All of the entertainment was either Filipino or Korean, and once in a while Vietnamese. They usually sang in English, but they didn't speak it. On a scale of one to ten, I would have rated the entertainment about a three and only because there were decent-looking females in the acts.

One of the more popular songs was "Joy to the World," which began with the words, "Jeremiah was a bull frog." But it came out minus the R's, so it was "Jeomia was a bullfog." Another one I'll always remember was Creedence Clearwater

Revival's, "Proud Mary." The refrain was "rolling down the river." I can hardly stand to hear those songs today without closing my eyes and seeing a Filipino group "olin down the ivea."

So with poor entertainment mixed into a touchy group of boozed-up GIs, we had a storm brewing frequently.

I remember one night when everyone must have been pissed off because there were fights breaking out frequently. At one point, one of the managers came up to me and asked me to control my men.

"I'm only a friend, not their commander," I told him. "If I do anything it will probably be to help them. They deserve a little fun."

He threw up his hands and said, "If anyone get hurt, it isn't my fault."

I sat back down and ordered beer for everyone at the table. Two of the men were on their favorite subject which was the easy time that the Air Force and Navy had. The topic that evening was how they had gotten past the AP the night before and had gone to the Air Force enlisted men's living area. They had found that there were women living in and cleaning the hootch area for little or nothing.

"Man, if you get caught there, the colonel will hang you out to dry," I said. I had been out of the bush long enough to forget the old standard answer.

"What are they gonna do, Red Pecker?" one of them asked. "Send me to Vietnam? The airmen don't have any choice but to share, or we'll blow their operation. We'll tear them apart and go back to the bush."

"We know what's up north," the other chimed in. "So we're gonna enjoy this while we can, whatever the cost."

I laughed and agreed.

"Just remember to leave your weapons at headquarters," I said.

That night, at about 10:30, several fights were going on,

so I left. As I crawled into my jeep, I could hear glass breaking, and the noise of the band was louder because of the fighting.

They're having a good time tonight, I thought.

There were a few grunts in the shadows, probably with a few girls, and it just supported the old theory about a soldier. If there was a girl within a hundred miles, not one, but all the grunts would know about it.

When I returned to camp, the colonel was looking for a particular lieutenant, so I offered to find him. I headed for the officers' club, but he wasn't there, so, on a hunch, I headed for the Air Force enlisted men's area.

I started walking the streets. It was quite a sight. There were dozens of Army, Navy, and Air Force men standing around smoking and joking. No one was trying to hide anything.

I asked a few grunts if they'd seen a Lieutenant X.

"Five hootches down, in the back," one directed me.

When I reached the fifth hootch, I walked in and surprised several guys and gals in various positions. They didn't seem to mind, but I was embarrassed to death.

I considered the situation, then started walking around the huts, peeking through the louvers and screen. At the seventh hootch I thought I recognized him. So I spoke through the screen.

Maybe I differed from the average guy, but if I'd been pumping along in the throes of sex and someone had called my name, I'd have been finished, right on the spot. But not this guy. He never missed a lick.

"I'll be done in a minute," he called.

During the ten minutes I waited, I took in the sights. They bordered on the ridiculous. From the air, it had to have looked like an anthill. Soldiers were coming and going, in and out. Girls were coming and going. downtown Chicago on the twenty-fourth of December couldn't have been busier.

Finally the lieutenant came out. On the way back, I ribbed him about catching VD, and he said that the Air Force took care of the girls.

"Once a week, they take the girls over to the hospital," he explained. "They check them out and give them all shots. A few bad ones sneak in, but if you talk to an airman, he'll point out the safe ones."

There was a saying in Vietnam that held that every woman had either VD or TB. "If they cough, fuck 'em!" was the rule of the day.

When we got back to headquarters, the lieutenant was mad as hell. The colonel had wanted a fourth for bridge.

"Next time, just ask me," I told the colonel. "I'm a little rusty, but I enjoy bridge and would be glad to fill in."

I watched them play for a while.

"What are your plans for tomorrow?" the colonel asked.

"I think I'll go down to the meat market and watch for a while," I answered.

"Meat market?"

"There's a place where all the village women come to," I explained. "The MPs keep them in a confined area. The concertina wire is three layers high and there's an MP station on each end. The grunts line up on one side of the wire and the women line up on the other. The men look them over, and when they pick one out, they walk down to the MP station and turn in their ID badges. Then they're free to do as they wish until the women's curfew.

"I guess it's quite a sight," I added. "There's a bushy area about fifty yards away, and they say you can't walk without stepping on bare behinds."

"Why are you going?" he asked.

"Just to see the sights."

"Our VD rate back at Evans was about 2 percent," he said. "But down here, it's up to 19 percent and rising every day."

"I know. I talked to Lieutenant Grisswald (our battalion medical officer), and he said at least 50 percent of the men have been in for shots at one time or another."

"The bad part is that the men don't realize they have a problem until they return to the bush," I continued. "We have to send a chopper out to bring them in for shots. Then we have to take them back. Some of the men have had more needles in their ass than a porcupine."

"Starting tomorrow, the meat market is off limits," he ordered.

"That's a good order, but I'll bet a steak supper stateside that it'll be disobeyed."

"It's a bet," he said.

Colonel Steverson owes me a steak supper, and I'm still waiting to collect.

The next morning, I drove the jeep down to the meat market. I parked on a hill just above the marketplace. What I witnessed that morning was unbelievable. There must have been three hundred women waiting at the wire.

I got out the binoculars and watched. The GI would go up to the wire carrying a poncho, blanket, or whatever he could fine to lay on the ground. He would walk along the wire, and the girls would make provocative gestures to him. When he picked one out, he would point at her, and about six women standing close by would assume it was them.

I laughed and thought of all the animal mating films I had seen in ag classes. There was one about the ritual of two swans ducking their heads and almost dancing. Well, this wasn't as graceful as that, but no film I ever saw was as funny as the scene I was watching.

The GI would point at one, and six or more would jump up and down, pointing at themselves, saying, "Me, me, me!" He would then go through several gestures, and more pointing, until finally they would get to the proper girl. Both would head for the MP station, and after turning in their ID cards, they would start for the bushes.

I trained my binoculars to the bushes and noticed that when the urge to mate came along, modesty, in many cases, vanished.

A few tried to hide, but most of them just found a blank area and had at it like two animals in heat.

About five seconds to five minutes later, they would sit and look at each other as if to say, "What do we do now?" Some times they would switch partners or take pictures of each other in all kinds of positions. Just let your imagination go, and it was happening.

Now I don't want anyone to get the idea that I was a goody-two-shoes or a pervert for watching, but if you had seen what I saw, I'll bet you would have watched just like I did. As for me not savoring in the fun, had I been a private and unmarried, I suspect my ass would have been constantly sore from the penicillin shots.

I was about to turn twenty-five in a few days, and besides, after Mike got killed, I had a bad taste in my mouth just being around any dinks, regardless of sex. I had seen dead men, women, and children, all with the same slant-eyed look. The last thing I needed was intimacy with a Vietnamese. So since there were no round-eyed girls around, I remained faithful to wife and country.

Just before R-and-R with my wife, I had one experience that scared me to death, and I sure didn't need another. Right after Lam Son 719, I noticed an itch on the head of my ying-yang.

I'd been born in a farmhouse, and none of us kids had been circumcised. One day, in the rear, I skinned 'er back and took a good look, and on the foreskin was a bunch of tiny things that looked like seed warts.

I went to see Doc Fredstrom, our battalion doctor. He told me I had venereal warts.

I just about fainted. After all the movies the Army had shown me on VD, I could just see my favorite friend dropping off.

"You'll have to fly down to Da Nang and see a specialist," he told me.

I hopped a shit-hook down to Da Nang.

I walked into the hospital ward, and a beautiful Army lieutenant nurse was standing there. I asked to see a certain doctor.

"What for?" she asked.

"I just need to see him," I repeated.

"No one sees a doctor until I okay it," she told me.

Now she could have been a Playboy pin-up girl, so I was a little nervous. But I behaved like a good soldier.

"Lady, I've got warts on the end of my pecker, and I just flew two hundred miles to have someone tell me how to get rid of them."

Suddenly, a siren went off and red lights started flashing. I was left standing there. A grunt squad had stepped on several booby traps and was on its way in.

I stood and watched as they brought in the first man.

You have to realize that a grunt from the jungle was already filthy and in rags. When he was placed on a rolling stretcher with white sheet, the contrast was eye-opening.

The first man was rushed down the line, and curtains were pulled around him. The second and third men came in, one minus a foot, and one minus an arm. When the ninth person came in, I stopped watching and went outside for a while.

I smoked and thought about it. I decided that booby traps were the worst enemy. If nothing else, they got to our minds. A man could be as careful as possible and still make that one mistake, the inevitable, sickening, body-rending mistake.

I sat around for three hours and finally the noise inside died down. I returned to the same nurse. She no longer had even a hint of a smile. She sent me down the hallway to the super-duper-pecker-checker. I went into his little cubbyhole and sat down. He looked cheerful enough.

"According to Doc Fredstrom, I have a problem," I began. "He said I have VD, and I don't know how I got it because I haven't touched a woman."

"Why didn't they just give you shots?" he inquired.

"Doc, I got warts on my pecker, and shots won't help that,"

I told him, fearing an advanced stage of some rare strain of venereal disease.

He laughed until his sides must have hurt. I didn't see anything funny at all. He had me show him, and again he laughed.

"Doc, I'm going to see my wife before long, and I don't know how I'm going to explain VD."

"You don't have VD," he chuckled. "Those are venereal warts. Did your doctor explain them to you?"

"Nope. He only said I had venereal warts. And I figured the only way to get them was from VD."

"You got the warts from being dirty. They are called venereal warts because of their location. They have absolutely nothing to do with any kind of venereal disease."

Now that I felt 100 percent better, I started laughing. This would just be another joke about a man's manhood.

"Doc, you just saved me. But how do I get rid of them?"

"Would you like to be circumcised on a Navy ship? You could get at least two weeks of good food and clean beds."

"What other alternatives do I have?"

He smiled and handed me a little bottle of liquid.

"Use it for one week and they'll go away. Just put a drop on each wart, wait about ten minutes, and then wash it off. And be sure to wash it off, or you'll be sorry.

"Your two weeks of R-and-R on a ship sounds good, but my M-16 and I need to get back up north in the mountains as soon as possible."

I don't think he understood my inner feelings. After having seen the wounded come in, I wondered where my platoon was, and if the men were all safe.

I stopped by a real flush toilet and put a few drops on, and waited about ten minutes, then washed it off. There was no pain whatsoever.

This is a piece of cake, I thought. Then I got on the shit-hook and landed at Phu Bai to spend the night. I applied the liquid again, leaving it on for thirty minutes, and it still didn't hurt.

The next day at Evans I applied it at bedtime and left it on. When I woke up the next morning, I had a cheery red pecker that hurt to touch.

As long as I didn't move, it didn't hurt.

I finally got my pants on. I was about to cry from the brush of the fatigues. It felt like someone had branded the end of it.

I decided from that point on that if the doctor said ten minutes, he meant ten minutes. By the next day it was a lot better. I returned to the bush, minus all the seed warts, vowing to keep my privates a little cleaner. And I didn't mean Pfcs.

17

I was sitting around my hootch one night when I heard someone say, "Delta Company, Second Platoon, has movement!" I moved over to headquarters to listen. The platoon had split into squads, and one squad had lights coming toward it. They appeared to be flashlights.

Sergeant Hill was in charge, and he was talking to Lieutenant Joy on the radio. They talked for about fifteen minutes.

One must realize that whenever anyone saw trouble, the whole world was monitoring the transmission. The Air Force planes, gunships, Navy, artillery, the colonel—everybody wanted to get in on the action. There was no additional activity that night, so everyone was keyed in on Sergeant Hill and Lieutenant Joy. I wasn't sure who ordered the gunships, but it was the first mistake.

The lights kept getting closer to the seven-man squad.

The gunships finally arrived. They made their first pass and identified themselves. The normal procedure was for the squad to identify itself by smoke or reflector shield (illumination shield), but the illumination cloth wasn't available.

The next thing that should have been used was a strobe light. I knew that some of the men had them.

But the pilot suggested trip flares.

That was the second mistake. A trip flare gave off a white light just like a flashlight. It was easy to distinguish the difference on the ground, but from a helicopter it was a lot harder.

The first pilot flew over and couldn't distinguish between friend and enemy and did not fire. But the second pilot was a cherry. He zeroed in on the trip flares with his rockets and blew the seven-man squad to pieces in one pass.

Sergeant Hill began to scream for medics over and over.

I ran to my jeep and sped for the Air Force hospital. I never stopped completely at the AP gate, but just yelled, "Incoming wounded!" and drove on.

I got there just as they were unloading the first bird. There were four men; two were declared dead on arrival. The other two were Charlie Kress, minus an arm, and Kenny Evenson, shot in the rear.

Kenny wasn't saying anything, but Charlie was saying over and over that the Army would pay forever.

I didn't recognize the two bodies. I figured they were some of the men who had transferred in.

"Can anyone identify the bodies?" someone asked.

"I might be able to," I said.

I got up really close and didn't recognize either man. One man was black, but I knew it couldn't have been Tyler. I pulled out his billfold and read the name Rodgers. I'd never met him.

I figured the other man was a transfer as well. But when I grabbed his billfold, I almost fainted.

It was Floyd Kotewa. In death it didn't look like Floyd at all. I was shell-shocked.

The second bird came in. Sergeant Hill had been hit in the leg, but he was walking. Jim Loughan was hit in the shoulder, ass, and foot, but managed to get around with the help of Brent Burford.

Loughan was taken on in. Burford and Hill stayed out with me.

"What in the hell happened, Sergeant?" I asked.

He told me his version. He didn't know who ordered the gunships.

"Lieutenant, I knew it was wrong, but we couldn't stop it," he shook his head.

I asked Burford what had happened. His story was similar.

"Lieutenant, I knew what was going to happen, so I hid behind a tree until it was over. Kress has a tape recording of everything that happened."

He then realized that he was the only one who hadn't been hurt. Two dead, four wounded, and one unhurt. It didn't seem right, but there wasn't much that seemed right in a war zone. Charlie Kress was fairly short, as were Evenson and Kotewa. But shortness didn't stop bullets or rockets from messing up lives.

The colonel showed up and told the doctors not to let anyone talk to the men. An investigation had already begun.

"Fix them up and keep them separate for a while," the colonel said.

I don't think any of the men realized I was there that night. It was understandable.

The next morning I went over to the hospital to see the men and was refused entry by two MPs. I went to Colonel Steverson, who was getting ready to go to the hospital himself. I asked to go along and was refused.

"Colonel, those are my men, and I want to see them."

"Later. For now, they're to be questioned about what happened."

"It was an accident," I told him.

It was determined that the pilot was at fault. I don't know if they did anything to him. It would be punishment enough just carrying the guilt for the rest of his life.

Sergeant Hill would be okay. Charlie Kress lost his arm just below the elbow. Kenny Evenson lost a hunk out of his ass. Jim Loughan had some serious wounds, but all would heal. His foot was bad, but the doctor assured me he would get used to it and hardly notice it.

Watching a Cobra gunship in action made a person realize how lucky the five who lived really were. A Cobra could put shrapnel in every square foot of a football field in one pass. I don't know how many rockets the pilot fired that night, but he was right on top of the flares.

I didn't get a chance to visit with the men after that because I received new orders. I was going home in forty days.

18

On September 10, 1971, I received my "early-out" orders. I was going home on October 21 instead of January 1. I had forty days left, and about seven of them were to be spent in transit and ETSing out of Uncle Sam's Army.

It was time to move the battalion back up north, and once again I was busy as a beaver getting everything planned and ready for the move. All went smoothly, and I woke up in my old cot back at Evans.

Only fourteen days left in-country.

A captain signed in to take my place. I had virtually nothing to do but hack around the rear area.

The monsoon season was upon us and it was totally miserable. The men in the jungle were worse off. I didn't know most of them because of all the transfers. Since I'd been in S-4, I had lost contact with all my friends from the bush, other than a few lieutenants who were leaving about a week after I was.

I played bridge with the colonel every night. I knew that I'd survived Vietnam. The days and nights were mental anguish to me, knowing that a chapter in my life was closing. The war was lost and had been from the beginning. Plans were being made to turn more and more over to the Vietnamese. Attitudes were changing.

However, I was going home at the right time. I resolved myself to that one fact. I doubted that I'd have been very happy had I been in-country when everything was being turned over to Charlie. Anyone could see that after we were gone, it would only be a few short months until the NVA controlled all of Vietnam.

The short-timer Pfcs and SP-4s from the bush were usually given rear duty for three weeks to get them out of the field. Some of their details were simple, but some were as deadly as being in the bush. One assignment that described the danger was minesweeping the roads. The grunts from the rear would walk guard for the minesweepers.

A man from our outfit named Barbi had nine days left in-country. Some asshole's idea of security was to walk the infantry down the side of the road with the minesweeper behind them.

Barbi was walking point for the security team. He was twenty meters ahead of the minesweepers when he stepped on one hundred pounds of TNT.

When they got him to the Eighty-fifth Evacuation Hospital, they realized that from the waist down there was nothing. They shoved the vital organs up as high as they could and sewed him up. He lived for three days.

I went over to see him and in some ways I wish I never had, but in others I'm glad I did. They kept him drugged so that he suffered as little as possible. But he wanted to live and go home. He was aware of his condition, yet he still wanted to live. The doctors and nurses were amazed that he lived for a few seconds, let alone three days, but he did.

I took my M-16 and went over to the minesweeping company and had a heated discussion with their colonel. I'm still a little ashamed of my behavior, but I accomplished what I had in mind.

From that day on, they filled trailers with sandbags, built shields around the drivers, and backed the trucks down the roads. It was a whole lot safer, and quicker as well.

Minesweeping was handled differently all over Vietnam. I don't claim to know anything about it, but any damned fool should have known better than to walk men first with minesweeper behind. It was suicide.

Barbi became known as the half man for a while. It was said that no man valued life more than he did.

Dan Brown signed in one day, I remembered him from college at Southern Illinois. I helped him settle in and taught him how to pack a ruck. I felt sorry for Dan because of what he was going to experience. He was a replacement for one of the lieutenants in the field. He would learn what the jungle was like, and then he'd go through the agony of standing down and turning every thing over to the ARVNs.

I told Dan what little I could. I felt he was going to make it because he was sharp enough, but back in the bush, each man had to meet the challenge alone. Each platoon was different, each captain was different, and each area of operation was different.

Combat is a funny thing. Nobody can look at a man and know how he will react. Sometimes the least likely soldier will be the best. Size, weight, agility, or intelligence didn't make anyone a soldier when the bullets started flying. Until someone had actually come under fire, a person just never knew.

I'm happy to say Dan Brown made it.

The drug problem had reached an all-time high in the Third, 187th. We were sending an average of two or three men per week to the dry-out areas. One required cold turkey for three weeks; the other was a more clinical area where extreme cases were treated.

Up until this point, I had noticed that all people I had recommended for promotion and medals had never received them. Except for Doc Wilson, nothing I had recommended had gone through. So with time on my hands, I checked out the clerk who handled the paper work.

I knew on sight that he was hooked on heroin. He even had open sores on his face which he unknowingly kept open by picking at them. I found his desk drawers full of undone paper work.

He lived solely for another shot of junk. How he managed to keep his job was amazing. Everyone seemed to ignore the drug problem as if it would go away. The men who were hooked took care of each other and looked unfavorably on anyone who tried to interfere.

Heroin was 90 percent pure, easy to get, and very cheap. A five-dollar purchase would last from one to three days, depending on the severity of the habit. Stateside, that would have been a hundred dollars a day or more.

When a man got short, he got a little tight and testy. It didn't matter what the rank; he felt he knew what was best for his safety. I didn't want to die because of a drug addict, so I let the knowledge slide for a few days.

They always had a going-home party for the staff officers. Although I was only a lieutenant, the colonel liked me and said I deserved the party, especially since I'd done a captain's job for ninety days.

The format was what some would call a fry. Each man got a chance to praise my work or jokingly cut me down. Since I was a junior officer to everyone in the room, we all had a fun time. When the colonel spoke, he spent about fifteen minutes telling everyone about my scrounging ability, and he really poured on the praise.

When he was finished, it was my turn, I thanked everybody and then laid into the colonel about the promotions and medals.

"Colonel, I never thought I would say this, and up till now it didn't matter, but suddenly I want those medals that my men and I deserve."

I explained several cases that I had written up about which nothing had ever been done.

"I've heard enough," he interrupted. "Your old platoon, as well as the whole battalion, will be taken care of ASAP."

I had no idea if I even had any medals coming, but for some reason, all the paper work began to get straightened out. The man with the sores on his face was sent to the extreme drug rehabilitation center, and within my last week, all the paper work had been straightened out, except for my own.

My last day.

As I was leaving, the colonel shook my hand and then hugged me.

"You earned everything," he told me. "I will see to it that by the time you are home all will be squared away."

I got on my first freedom bird, a shit-hook to Da Nang. I was really torn between the happiness of going home and the sadness of leaving friends, not knowing if they'd live or die.

I still had my leech straps on, and I carried a small duffel bag full of memories. There were a set of jungle clothes, my personal case, and three souvenirs inside: a Russian-made watch and two homemade knives.

At Da Nang, all the guys who were going home were put in one area. The first day was very upsetting. The MPs tried to take my jungle fatigues from me, but I refused to give them up. Finally, they let me keep the fatigues and issued me some khaki clothes to wear home.

The last step was the drug test. Each man had to piss in a cup so they could analyze it. If he'd taken any drugs up to thirty-six hours earlier, they would show up in the urine.

I hadn't thought much about it, except that it made me mad to think I wasn't trusted on my word. Several of the men looked awful in the face and acted upset. Then I realized that if a guy was addicted, he couldn't go thirty-six hours straight

If a person flunked the test, he had to be tested thoroughly, which could have taken two weeks. If he was addicted, it could have been longer still. I thought I could have named my price. One good piss would have made me a lot of money. But even if I'd have been serious, the MPs watched us every second.

It was very degrading going through the test. But when I realized that close to half of those men showed signs of withdrawal or nervousness, and since I had never taken any kind of drugs, and not even smoked one joint of Mary Jane, I wasn't concerned, as long as they kept my urine specimen straight. I told the medical sergeant to protect my sample with his life.

They wrote the names on each plastic cup to keep them straight. All I knew for sure was that I passed the test. I had no way of knowing how many didn't. My guess was that several didn't pass, but it was for their own benefit, whether they realized it or not.

I put on my khakis the next day. All we had left was to pick up our paper work and pass customs. Then we'd be freedom bound. Back to the world.

Soldiers had come from all over the country, and I didn't know anyone. They checked out everything and gave us body frisks. The soldier in front of me had a small Sony television. They took the back off and let a dog smell it. We went through three narcotic dogs before boarding the plane.

The guy in front of me had Army OD green D-cell batteries in his Sony, and they took them. It was legitimate, but with all the millions of dollars that were wasted daily, I thought it was pretty cheap to take four D-cell batteries because they were unauthorized. Besides, they'd been used and were no good to anyone. Maybe the custom man needed some for his Sony.

When it was my turn, I dumped out my duffel bag, and the

guy grabbed the two knives immediately. He looked at the watch.

"All this should have been turned in for intelligence."

"Buddy, it already has been," I snarled. "It was given back to me."

He gave me a long line of bullshit about the paper work I didn't have.

"You can't take them home."

"Look man, they are souvenirs, and I am taking them home."

"Step out of line and get the proper paper work, Lieutenant, and you can keep them."

I stepped out of the line and asked an MP how to get the paper work. His answer upset me to no end.

"Lieutenant, it would take about two days to get it all done. Maybe longer. Once your freedom bird is full, you will have to wait until tomorrow, anyway."

I made a quick decision and handed the custom man my two knives and watch.

"I hope you tell a lot of war stories to your kids about how you captured those because there is no good reason not to let me keep them, unless you want them."

He gave me a dirty look.

I stomped to the freedom bird.

I took as aisle seat and waited for the bird to fill up. I realized how glad I was to be going home and back to the farm.

A loud cheer went up when the bird first took off, and it was to be that way every time we landed and took off.

It was dark when we finally landed in Seattle. It sure wasn't the homecoming I'd expected. They herded us like cattle into a sleeping area. If we'd arrived at the proper mealtime, I think we would have gotten a steak, but we arrived at a late hour.

I was directed to an officers' sleeping area. There must have been twenty-five or thirty lieutenants there. We went to sleep about 1:30 A.M. and were awakened at 4 A.M. I never slept because I wasn't used to the bed. I had gotten used to an army cot, having been a REMF for ninety days, but it still wasn't the same.

Since there were so many officers, they informed us that they could process us out early and run us through before the enlisted men were up and around. We all agreed quickly, and after breakfast we started the final stage of ETSing out of the Army.

All the paper work we'd done coming into the service had to be redone or finalized. My medals were presented to me. I had no idea what I had coming or what I was to do with them, but they showed us, and we pinned them on hurriedly.

The last thing, at about 10 A.M., was our reenlistment talk. When we were all seated, the sergeant told us that most of us would have to take an enlisted man's rank of E-6 because of the large number of lieutenants.

"Only a few of you will be selected to stay as officers ... I assume you just want to go home."

We all cheered. He said we were dismissed unless we wanted to talk with him. We ran out of there like a covey of quail.

Four of us grabbed a taxi to the airport. We all had money to get home on. I had five hundred dollars extra.

Upon arrival at the airport, we literally ran to the ticket counters, and there was a plane leaving for Chicago in five minutes. They were closing the door as I boarded.

When I sat down, it all hit me. I was a civilian and it was all over. I was sure there was a glow about me.

Everyone around me was civilian, going about their business as if there was no war going on anywhere. In the four-hour flight to Chicago, I realized that I didn't even know what airport I'd flown out of.

I hadn't notified my family that I was coming home. Because of my early-out, I'd decided to just show up and surprise everyone. I didn't know what being high on drugs was like, but I was beginning to feel like part of the clouds.

I began to realize that I'd survived. It really began to sink in just where I'd been and what I'd done. I wanted to talk to someone, but civilians didn't seem to notice I was there. I still wonder whether they knew I was fresh from Vietnam. I really believe that my appearance caused them to clam up and refuse to discuss anything. I didn't want to talk about Vietnam, but I could have loved to talk about current events, farming, or hunting. Anything but silence.

I was a survivor.

I had been to war, yet there I sat, in a plane on my way home, and no one seemed to realize I was there.

I shuffled though my papers, trying to pass the time. I found the paper work on my medals and began to read about myself.

I'd received three Bronze Stars, one with a valor device, and one Air Medal for combat assaults. A person had to have had twenty-five combat assaults to receive one. I had made forty-nine.

I also received one Army Commendation Medal and two unit citations from the Vietnamese for Lam Son 719. I found out later that anyone who had served in Vietnam received the commendation medal, and, if he'd kept his nose clean, one Bronze Star. There were also two medals for serving in Vietnam.

A person could get a big head very easily if he read the paper work that accompanied a medal. Colonel Steverson had assured me that the paper work would catch up, and he'd been right.

I hadn't wanted any medals when I went overseas, but they suddenly meant something to me. I was a survivor. I had proof. The Combat Infantry Badge could only be won by a grunt who had served in a combat zone. I was on a high in that airplane that was indescribable.

I was smoking a cigarette and engrossed in my reading when a stewardess asked me to extinguish the smoke because we were approaching Chicago. I finished it, anyway, and got the first attention I'd had on the whole flight.

At O'Hare Airport, I grabbed a taxi to the train station. It was 6:15 P.M. when I arrived, and the place was closing down. When I left home there were trains coming and going twenty-four hours a day, but when I needed one the most, I was told I had to wait until six o'clock the next morning.

I talked to a janitor. He informed me that it wasn't safe to spend the night alone at the station.

I told him I'd slept in worse places and could see no sense in a motel bill for one night. "Besides," I said, "I just came home from Vietnam. I'm not the least bit scared."

"You would be the first the gangs would pick on," he said. "Vietnam veterans aren't too highly thought of."

His response startled me.

I walked around until 8 P.M. and the janitor's words kept eating at me. Why would anyone pick on me? All I wanted was to go home.

At about nine o'clock, the shadows began to bother me. I realized I didn't have a friend or a weapon to protect myself. It didn't seem right, but I decided a hotel might be the best idea.

There was a decent-looking hotel about three blocks away, so I headed for it. My high was over, and I was dog-tired when I asked for a room.

The desk clerk asked me if I had the money for a room. I just about exploded. "I just got back from Vietnam and hell yes, I have the money!" I growled.

"It'll have to be in advance. We have to watch you veterans closely or you sneak off without paying."

"It seems to me that a veteran ought to get a free room instead of bad lip from a desk clerk."

"Pay up or I'll call the police."

I thought about it for a few seconds and then paid him for the night.

"If you want room service, it's gotta be cash, or no deliver," he told me, as if he hadn't said enough already.

If I hadn't have been so tired and anxious to get home. I

would have let him call the police just to see what would have happened. No one had spoken a kind word to me for several hours. I was beginning to feel like a freak.

I sat around for a while and finally realized there was a TV in the room. I hadn't watched TV in almost a year, unless it had been in Hawaii. I turned to the ten o'clock news. Vietnam was almost one-third of the show. The casualty counts seemed to be the main topic.

I ordered some food from room service and settled into an old Tarzan movie. I woke up in the chair at 4 A.M., then showered, shaved, and headed for the lobby at 5 A.M.

I threw the key on the desk.

"I should get my money back," I snapped at the same guy. "All I used was a chair and the TV."

He checked to see if I had any charges to the room.

"Okay. You can leave, sir. And please come back."

It'll be a cold day in hell before I return, I thought.

On the way to the train station, I began to feel good again. At about noon I would be in Mattoon, only thirty miles from home and some friendly people.

The ticket agent opened up at 6 A.M. but the train didn't leave until 8 A.M., so I was the only one there to buy a ticket.

"Are you on leave?" the agent asked.

"No way," I answered. "I'm on my way home for good."

"I'm a World War II veteran," he told me.

I thought I'd found an understanding soul at last, but I was wrong. We talked for almost ten minutes before I realized he was talking down to me.

"I get the impression that you don't think I deserve the title of veteran," I said.

"It wasn't a war," he said. "Just a conflict. Besides, you young guys don't have the discipline it takes to be soldiers."

"Man, I've been in the jungle, I've been shot at, lost my best friend, and watched the suffering of several more. And I did it for my country, be it right or wrong. I'm a veteran."

"Well, you're one of the few who might be qualified," he allowed, realizing I'd gotten a little heated. "But the majority don't deserve it."

If there hadn't have been bars between us I would have struck him with my left fist, just to make a point. But again, I walked away madder than a wet hen and waited for the train.

An hour later, I was on the train and glad to be leaving Chicago. A young couple sat down across from me. Finally, someone wanted to talk. They were newlyweds and were headed for Southern Illinois University in Carbondale.

We spent the next three hours talking about Vietnam. The right or wrong of it. I wasn't happy about the topic, but at least they weren't offensive about it. The young man had drawn a high lottery number and was happy because the odds were in his favor.

"You're lucky," I agreed. "If you don't have to go, so be it."

He thought that I meant our efforts in Vietnam were negative.

"I'm glad to see you agree," he said.

"I'm not negative about our country being there at all," I clarified. "All I'm saying is you're lucky, that's all."

This went on for three hours. I was glad to get off the train in Mattoon.

I walked to Route 16 to hitch a free ride to Charleston, ten miles away. From there, I just knew I could catch a ride to Casey. Charleston was a college town and there were several hometown people who worked there.

I waited for a ride for two hours, but everyone just drove on by. I couldn't believe that no one would stop. I was in uniform. Nobody even slowed down.

I noticed a crowd down the street, so I walked over to see what was going on. It was a Masonic Lodge and they were serving a turkey dinner. I hadn't eaten since my room service, so I walked inside.

At that time, I was a third-degree Mason from Clark Lodge 603 in Martinsville, so I knew there would be friends inside. They never asked any questions, just sat me down and fed me. They didn't know I was a Mason, and none of them knew me personally, but I was treated well because I was a serviceman. And that was all they needed to know to make a man feel at home.

They don't realize it today, but they were the first friendly people I met on my trip home. I was offered a ride to Charleston, but I refused. I just knew I could get a ride so easily. But by 2 P.M., I was still standing on Route 16.

A taxi pulled up.

"What'll it cost to ride to Charleston?" I asked.

"Ten bucks."

I hopped in.

"Where are you headed?" he asked along the way.

"Home to Casey."

"Why didn't you call family to come get you?"

"I got this close and I wanted to surprise my family. They don't know I'm coming, so it'll be a surprise for everyone."

He dumped me on Route 130. I'd no more than gotten out when my wife's cousin drove by and recognized me. She took me straight to the place where my wife worked. From there, it was back to the farm in Casey.

I was home where I belonged, and yet I was torn inside for some reason that I couldn't explain.

Epilogue

As I look back on my experiences in the military and especially to the time I spent in Vietnam, I realize how young and vulnerable we were.

There were many problems during the later years of the war, and though I witnessed most of the problems, I did not feel qualified to elaborate on some of them. I mentioned the drug abuse, but I found it difficult to speak about the reasons drugs were used.

However, it should be noted that in Vietnam drugs were used by the local people, and they were readily available at a low cost. Being eighteen to twenty-one years of age was one reason to experience those things tabooed by society—especially in circumstances of war. The pressure of being in a life-threatening situation caused some men to seek the bottle while others captured a few moments of bliss through drugs. Death paranoia was another explanation for drug abuse. Some men felt they wouldn't survive, so they lived for the moment and didn't look to the future. Family problems back home, wives, girlfriends, society pressures, no job, no education, being drafted and then waking up in Vietnam were all reasons for irrational behavior.

But it is sad for people to view all Vietnam veterans as people who have experienced hard drugs. Many soldiers never yielded to the temptations, and to use the war as the only reason for those who did is also sad and incorrect.

Another problem which plagued me was the racial tension

that was prevalent in our unit. Only now, after years of thought and experience, do I feel comfortable in understanding the problems the young blacks had in the sixties and early seventies.

I was afraid to address the racial issue in the manuscript for fear of coming across as prejudiced and depicting the blacks' role in Vietnam as more bad than good. I still cannot condone some blacks' attitudes, yet I can sympathize with and understand some of the problems.

However, many of the blacks fought side by side with their buddies. Color meant absolutely nothing in the jungle. Dependence on your fellow soldier for your life crossed all color barriers. Mexican-American, Indians, blacks, and whites fought and died for each other with no malice.

Once again, the rear areas seemed to be the source of the problem. In our outfit, a few blacks refused to fight and existed in the rear area as a gang or band that nobody knew what to do about. As a platoon leader, I didn't need that type of man in the field.

When blacks who did serve returned to the rear areas for rest, they were under constant pressure from both blacks and whites. There has to be a special place in this country's heart for those men who bypassed all prejudice and fought for their country as Americans, especially in the turmoil of the sixties and early seventies.

The drugs and the racial tension were probably the two biggest problems the Army faced. I grew to manhood and never knew a Mexican-American or a black personally; however, my experience in Vietnam taught me a form of prejudice that I would like to share.

I am German, French, English, and American Indian, but first of all I am an American. I believe in equality for all; equality is our Constitution. Color is not mentioned. If you love this country to the point of defending a few words written years ago, then you are a friend and fellow American. When a person does not live by our Constitution, his discontent awakens my prejudice. Black or white means nothing. Yes, there is prejudice in this country. Yes, there is inadequacy in our laws. But I ask you: Where else would you rather live? Had our forefathers not fought in all the wars, where would you be today? Black or white, what type of law would you be living under?

As an American, I love my country and respect my flag to the point that if war faces us again, I am prepared to defend—to the best of my ability—life, liberty, and the pursuit of happiness for the next generation.

Sincerely,

Donald E. Stephen
3733 E. Snake Trail Rd.
Martinsville, IL 62442

1 April 71

Dear Michael:

Happy April Fools Day! The day has dawned brightly here; the sun shining brightly and giving every indication that spring has arrived as last. You can't imagine how happy the prospects of spring and summer weather make me. I'm no lover of winter sports; I don't "think snow"; I much prefer the heat of the summer to the cold and discomfort of the winter.

The news indicates lots of action in your area—unless you have moved recently. We pray for your protection. No doubt you have moments of doubts and discouragement. But please don't give in to them. Be sustained in the belief that what you are doing is necessary. To back out of Vietnam is to back into some other country. The Russians won't have it any other way. They are testing our national resolve. This is a war of mind spirit and, despite the prophets of gloom and doom, we are winning it in the sense that South Vietnam is becoming a viable nation just as—with our help—South Korea became one in the fifties.

I am much amused—and chagrined also—by the anti-war protesters. I read in *Time* magazine (your subscription to me) that Russia has thirty-three divisions in various countries in Eastern Europe— satellite countries such as Poland, Hungary, Romania, Bulgaria, East Germany, etc. Never do I hear any protests about this intimidation of those sovereign nations. There have never—to my knowledge—been any demonstrations from the anti-war groups about Russia's invasion of Hungary or Czechoslovakia. When protesters give equal time to Russia's incursions into other countries—when they demand that Russian troops as well as American troops be pulled back—when they protest by mass demonstrations Russia's intransigence toward Russian Jews' attempts to immigrate to Israel—only then will I agree that it's time for us to leave Vietnam.

Many things are tops-turvy in this world. Just don't despair. Do your job to the best of your ability. Have compassion for the Vietnamese people. Don't see them as "gooks" or "slants" or "slopes"—but see them as God's own—in his image and likeness—with aspirations and hopes much the same as ours.

Love,
Dad

18 May 71

Dear Mr. President,

I hope this letter finds you and your family in good health and in contentment with your decisions as President of Our United States.

I am presently sitting in the steaming jungle of northern Military Region I, South Vietnam, with a few minutes of free time in which I thought I could use best by writing you a little note of encouragement.

As an infantry platoon leader, I think I can begin to appreciate the pressures, pains, and satisfactions of someone in the position of decision maker for literally millions of people.

I often think about and discuss with members of my platoon, the reasons for our existence here in Vietnam. As you can imagine, I find many varied opinions; some pro, some con.

I just want you to know that as far as I am concerned, thus far I believe that you are making the right decisions concerning our involvement in Vietnam. Naturally, I do not enjoy being here, nor do I enjoy in any way, the thought of war. However, I do understand the need for our presence here. Because I do understand and feel a moral obligation as an American to help defend this country against communism, I want you to know that this "G.I." is behind you, "All the Way."

I am enclosing a letter for you to read, written to me by my father. He says in precise terms, exactly how I feel about our involvement here. If I had his knowledge and command of the language, I would have said the same things.

In times as critical, challenging, and demanding as these, we all could use a little encouragement. I know that I often feel the need for it, and I'm sure that a man faced with your decisions most certainly needs some.

I hope this letter inspires and encourages you as it has me.

I wish you continued good health and good judgment, but most of all, I wish you God's blessing.

Respectfully yours,
First Lieutenant Michael M. Dalton
D/3/187/ 101 ABN. DIV
APO 96383

P.S. Please return my father's letter to me.

June 29, 1971

Dear Mr. Dalton:

As you can imagine, many letters come to me from parents noting correspondence from their soldier-sons, but I was particularly pleased to hear from your son Michael, recently which proudly enclosed one of your letters to him.

This is just a note to thank you and your family for the support you are giving my efforts to bring peace to southeast Asia. I was particularly moved by your thoughts concerning the Vietnamese people, and I know that the deep devotion to God, and the strong humanitarian concern that Michael learned in your home, must be a source of strength and inspiration for him as he serves overseas.

Michael wanted your letter back so I am returning it to you and I don't think Mike would mind my sending you the copy of his letter to me. I also thought you might like to see a copy of a speech I made at West Point recently. It touches on some of the items you and your son have discussed.

With my gratitude and best wishes to all the Daltons,

Sincerely,

Richard Nixon

Mr. Edward T. Dalton
536 Walcott Street
Pawtucket, Rhode Island